I0831312

EUGENE ONEGIN

A NOVEL IN VERSE

Eugene Onegin: A Novel in Verse
Pushkin, Alexander 1799 – 1837
First Published in 1833
Translated by Henry Joseph Spalding
Spalding, Henry Joseph 1840 – 1907
Translation published by Macmillan & Co in 1881

Text set in 18 point Helvetica.
Chapter headings set in Helvetica Neue.

ISBN: 978-1-83412-261-8

EUGENE ONEGIN

A NOVEL IN VERSE

ALEXANDER PUSHKIN

Translated from the Russian
by Lieut.-Col. [Henry] Spalding

GRAND TYPE CLASSICS

CONTENTS

Eugene Onegin: A Novel in Verse

Preface

EUGENE ONÉGUINE, the chief poetical work of Russia's greatest poet, having been translated into all the principal languages of Europe except our own, I hope that this version may prove an acceptable contribution to literature. Tastes are various in matters of poetry, but the present work possesses a more solid claim to attention in the series of faithful pictures it offers of Russian life and manners. If these be compared with Mr. Wallace's book on Russia, it will be seen that social life in that empire still preserves many of the characteristics which distinguished it half a century ago – the period of the first publication of the latter cantos of this poem.

Many references will be found in it to our own country and its literature. Russian poets have carefully plagiarized the English – notably Joukóvski. Pushkin, however, was no plagiarist, though undoubtedly his mind was greatly influenced by the genius of Byron – more especially in the earliest part of his career. Indeed, as will be remarked in the following pages, he scarcely makes an effort to disguise this fact.

The biographical sketch is of course a mere outline. I did not think a longer one advisable, as memoirs do not usually excite much interest till the subjects of them are pretty well known. In the "notes" I have endeavored to elucidate a somewhat obscure subject. Some of the poet's allusions remain enigmatical to the present day. The point of each sarcasm naturally passed out of mind together with the society against which it was levelled. If some of the versification is rough and wanting in "go," I must plead in excuse the difficult form of the stanza, and in many instances the inelastic nature of the subject matter to be versified. Stanza XXXV Canto II forms a good example of the latter difficulty, and is omitted in the German and French versions to which I have had access. The translation of foreign verse is comparatively easy so long as it is confined to conventional poetic subjects, but when it embraces abrupt scraps of conversation and the description of local customs it becomes a much more arduous affair. I think I may say that I have adhered closely to the text of the original.

The following foreign translations of this poem have appeared:

1. French prose. Oeuvres choisis de Pouchekine. H. Dupont. Paris, 1847.

2. German verse. A. Puschkin's poetische Werke. F. Bodenstedt. Berlin, 1854.

3. Polish verse. Eugeniusz Oniegin. Roman Aleksandra Puszkina. A. Sikorski. Vilnius, 1847.

4. Italian prose. Racconti poetici di A. Puschkin, tradotti da A. Delatre. Firenze, 1856.

London, May 1881.

Mon Portrait

WRITTEN BY the poet at the age of 15.

Vous me demandez mon portrait,
Mais peint d'après nature:
Mon cher, il sera bientot fait,
Quoique en miniature.

Je suis un jeune polisson
Encore dans les classes;
Point sot, je le dis sans façon,
Et sans fades grimaces.

Oui! il ne fut babillard
Ni docteur de Sorbonne,
Plus ennuyeux et plus braillard
Que moi-même en personne.

Ma taille, à celle des plus longs,
Elle n'est point egalée;
J'ai le teint frais, les cheveux blonds,
Et la tete bouclée.

J'aime et le monde et son fracas,
Je hais la solitude;
J'abhorre et noises et débats,
Et tant soit peu l'étude.

Spectacles, bals, me plaisent fort,
Et d'après ma pensee,
Je dirais ce que j'aime encore,
Si je n'étais au Lycée.

Après cela, mon cher ami,
L'on peut me reconnaître,

Mon Portrait

Oui! tel que le bon Dieu me fit,
Je veux toujours paraître.

Vrai dé1mon, par l'espiéglerie,
Vrai singe par sa mine,
Beaucoup et trop d'étourderie,
Ma foi! voilà Pouchekine.

Note: Russian proper names to be pronounced as in French (the nasal sound of m and n excepted) in the following translation. The accent, which is very arbitrary in the Russian language, is indicated unmistakably in a rhythmical composition.

A Short Biographical Notice of Alexander Pushkin

ALEXANDER SERGÉVITCH PUSHKIN was born in 1799 at Pskoff, and was a scion of an ancient Russian family. In one of his letters it is recorded that no less than six Pushkins signed the Charta declaratory of the election of the Románoff family to the throne of Russia, and that two more affixed their marks from inability to write.

In 1811 he entered the Lyceum, an

aristocratic educational establishment at Tsarskoe Selo, near St. Petersburg, where he was the friend and schoolmate of Prince Gortchakoff the Russian Chancellor. As a scholar he displayed no remarkable amount of capacity, but was fond of general reading and much given to versification. Whilst yet a schoolboy he wrote many lyrical compositions and commenced **Ruslan and Liudmila**, his first poem of any magnitude, and, it is asserted, the first readable one ever produced in the Russian language. During his boyhood he came much into contact with the poets Dmitrieff and Joukóvski, who were intimate with his father, and his uncle, Vassili Pushkin, himself an author of no mean repute. The friendship of the historian Karamzine must have exercised a still more beneficial influence upon him.

In 1817 he quitted the Lyceum and obtained an appointment in the Foreign Office at St. Petersburg. Three years of reckless dissipation in the capital, where his lyrical talent made him universally popular, resulted in 1818 in a putrid fever which was near carrying him off. At this period of his life he scarcely slept at all; worked all day and dissipated at night. Society was open to him from the palace of the prince to the officers' quarters of the Imperial Guard. The reflection of this mode of life may be noted in the first canto of **Eugene Onéguine** and the early dissipations of the "Philosopher just turned eighteen," – the exact age of Pushkin when he commenced his career in the Russian capital.

In 1820 he was transferred to the bureau of Lieutenant-General Inzoff, at Kishineff in Bessarabia. This event was probably due to his composing and privately circulating an "Ode to Liberty," though the attendant circumstances have never yet been thoroughly brought to light. An indiscreet admiration for Byron most likely involved the young poet in this scrape. The tenor of this production, especially its audacious allusion to the murder of the emperor Paul, father of the then reigning Tsar, assuredly deserved, according to aristocratic ideas, the deportation to Siberia which was said to have been prepared for the author. The intercession of Karamzine and Joukóvski procured a commutation of his sentence. Strangely enough, Pushkin appeared anxious to deceive the public as to the real cause of his sudden disappearance from the capital; for in an Ode to Ovid composed about this time he styles himself a "voluntary exile." (See Note 4 to this volume.)

During the four succeeding years he made numerous excursions amid the beautiful countries which from the basin of the Euxine – and amongst these the Crimea and the Caucasus. A nomad life passed amid the beauties of nature acted powerfully in developing his poetical genius. To this period he refers in the final canto of **Eugene Onéguine** (st. v.), when enumerating the various influences which had contributed to the formation of his Muse:

> "Then, the far capital forgot,
> Its splendour and its blandishments,
> In poor Moldavia cast her lot,
> She visited the humble tents
> Of migratory gipsy hordes," etc. etc.

During these pleasant years of youth he penned some of his most delightful poetical works: amongst these, **The Prisoner of the Caucasus, The Fountain of Baktchiserai**, and the **Gipsies**. Of the two former it may be said that they are in the true style of the **Giaour** and the **Corsair**. In fact, just at that point of time Byron's fame – like the setting sun – shone out with dazzling lustre and irresistibly charmed the mind of Pushkin amongst many others. The **Gipsies** is more original; indeed the poet himself has been identified with Aleko, the hero of the tale, which may well be founded on his own personal adventures without involving the guilt of a double murder. His undisguised admiration for Byron doubtless exposed him to imputations similar to those commonly levelled against that poet. But Pushkin's talent was too genuine for him to remain long subservient to that of another, and in a later period of his career he broke loose from all trammels and selected a line peculiarly his own. Before leaving this stage in our narrative we may point out the fact that during the whole of this period of comparative seclusion the poet was indefatigably occupied in study. Not only were the standard works of European literature perused, but two more languages – namely Italian and Spanish – were added to his original stock: French, English, Latin and German having been acquired at the Lyceum. To this happy union of literary research with the study of nature we must attribute the sudden bound by which he soon afterwards attained the pinnacle of poetic fame amongst his own countrymen.

In 1824 he once more fell under the imperial displeasure. A letter seized in the post, and expressive of atheistical sentiments (possibly but a transient vagary of his youth) was the ostensible cause of his banishment from Odessa to his paternal estate of Mikhailovskoe in the province of Pskoff. Some, however, aver that personal pique on the part of Count Vorontsoff, the Governor of Odessa, played a part in the transaction. Be this as it may, the consequences were serious for the poet, who was not only placed under the surveillance of the police, but expelled from the Foreign Office by express order of the Tsar "for bad conduct." A letter on this subject, addressed by Count Vorontsoff to Count Nesselrode, is an amusing instance of the arrogance with which stolid mediocrity frequently passes judgment on rising genius. I transcribe a portion thereof:

A Short Biographical Notice

Odessa, 28**th March** (7**th April**) 1824

Count – Your Excellency is aware of the reasons for which, some time ago, young Pushkin was sent with a letter from Count Capo d'Istria to General Inzoff. I found him already here when I arrived, the General having placed him at my disposal, though he himself was at Kishineff. I have no reason to complain about him. On the contrary, he is much steadier than formerly. But a desire for the welfare of the young man himself, who is not wanting in ability, and whose faults proceed more from the head than from the heart, impels me to urge upon you his removal from Odessa. Pushkin's chief failing is ambition. He spent the bathing season here, and has gathered round him a crowd of adulators who praise his genius. This maintains in him a baneful delusion which seems to turn his head – namely, that he is a "distinguished writer;" whereas, in reality he is but a feeble imitator of an author in whose favour very little can be said (Byron). This it is which keeps him from a serious study of the great classical poets, which might exercise a beneficial effect upon his talents – which cannot be denied him – and which might make of him in course of time a "distinguished writer."

The best thing that can be done for him is to remove him hence....

The Emperor Nicholas on his accession pardoned Pushkin and received him once more into favour. During an interview which took place it is said that the Tsar promised the poet that he alone would in future be the censor of his productions. Pushkin was restored to his position in the Foreign Office and received the appointment of Court Historian. In 1828 he published one of his finest poems, **Poltava**, which is founded on incidents familiar to English readers in Byron's **Mazeppa**. In 1829 the hardy poet accompanied the Russian army which under Paskevitch captured Erzeroum. In 1831 he married a beautiful lady of the Gontchareff family and settled in the neighbourhood of St. Petersburg, where he remained for the remainder of his life, only occasionally visiting Moscow and Mikhailovskoe. During this period his chief occupation consisted in collecting and investigating materials for a projected history of Peter the Great, which was undertaken at the express desire of the Emperor. He likewise completed a history of the revolt of Pougatchoff, which occurred in the reign of Catherine II. [Note: this individual having personated Peter III, the deceased husband of the Empress, raised the Orenburg Cossacks in revolt. This revolt was not suppressed without extensive destruction of life and property.] In 1833 the poet visited Orenburg, the scene of the dreadful excesses he recorded; the fruit of his journey being one of the most charming tales ever written, **The Captain's Daughter**. [Note: Translated in **Russian Romance**, by Mrs. Telfer, 1875.]

The remaining years of Pushkin's life, spent in the midst of domestic bliss and grateful literary occupation, were what lookers-on style "years of unclouded happiness." They were, however, drawing rapidly to a close. Unrivalled distinction rarely fails to arouse bitter animosity amongst the envious, and Pushkin's existence had latterly been embittered by groundless insinuations against his wife's reputation in the shape of anonymous letters addressed to himself and couched in very insulting language. He fancied he had traced them to one Georges d'Anthés, a Frenchman in the Cavalier Guard, who had been adopted by the Dutch envoy Heeckeren. D'Anthés, though he had espoused Madame Pushkin's sister, had conducted himself with impropriety towards the former lady. The poet displayed in this affair a fierce hostility quite characteristic of his African origin but which drove him to his destruction. D'Anthés, it was subsequently admitted, was not the author of the anonymous letters; but as usual when a duel is proposed, an appeal to reason was thought to smack of cowardice. The encounter took place in February 1837 on one of the islands of the Neva. The weapons used were pistols, and the combat was of a determined, nay ferocious character. Pushkin was shot before he had time to fire, and, in his fall, the barrel of his pistol became clogged with snow which lay deep upon the ground at the time. Raising himself on his elbow, the wounded man called for another pistol, crying, "I've strength left to fire my shot!" He fired, and slightly wounded his opponent, shouting "Bravo!" when he heard him exclaim that he was hit. D'Anthés was, however, but slightly contused whilst Pushkin was shot through the abdomen. He was transported to his residence and expired after several days passed in extreme agony. Thus perished in the thirty-eighth year of his age this distinguished poet, in a manner and amid surroundings which make the duel scene in the sixth canto of this poem seem almost prophetic. His reflections on the premature death of Lenski appear indeed strangely applicable to his own fate, as generally to the premature extinction of genius.

Pushkin was endowed with a powerful physical organisation. He was fond of long walks, unlike the generality of his countrymen, and at one time of his career used daily to foot it into St. Petersburg and back, from his residence in the suburbs, to conduct his investigations in the Government archives when employed on the History of Peter the Great. He was a good swordsman, rode well, and at one time aspired to enter the cavalry; but his father not being able to furnish the necessary funds he declined serving in the less romantic infantry. Latterly he was regular in his habits; rose early, retired late, and managed to get along with but very little sleep. On rising he betook himself forthwith to his literary occupations, which were continued till afternoon, when they gave place to physical exercise. Strange as it will appear to many, he preferred the autumn months, especially when rainy, chill and misty, for the production of his literary compositions, and was proportionally depressed by the approach of spring. (Cf. Canto VII st. ii.)

"Mournful is thine approach to me,
O Spring, thou chosen time of love," etc.

He usually left St. Petersburg about the middle of September and remained in the country till December. In this space of time it was his custom to develop and perfect the inspirations of the remaining portion of the year. He was of an impetuous yet affectionate nature and much beloved by a numerous circle of friends. An attractive feature in his character was his unalterable attachment to his aged nurse, a sentiment which we find reflected in the pages of **Eugene Onéguine** and elsewhere.

The preponderating influence which Byron exercised in the formation of his genius has already been noticed. It is indeed probable that we owe **Onéguine** to the combined impressions of **Childe Harold** and **Don Juan** upon his mind. Yet the Russian poem excels these masterpieces of Byron in a single particular – namely, in completeness of narrative, the plots of the latter being mere vehicles for the development of the poet's general reflections. There is ground for believing that Pushkin likewise made this poem the record of his own experience. This has doubtless been the practice of many distinguished authors of fiction whose names will readily occur to the reader. Indeed, as we are never cognizant of the real motives which actuate others, it follows that nowhere can the secret springs of human action be studied to such advantage as within our own breasts. Thus romance is sometimes but the reflection of the writer's own individuality, and he adopts the counsel of the American poet:

Look then into thine heart and write!

But a further consideration of this subject would here be out of place. Perhaps I cannot more suitably conclude this sketch than by quoting from his **Ode to the Sea** the poet's tribute of admiration to the genius of Napoleon and Byron, who of all contemporaries seem the most to have swayed his imagination.

Farewell, thou pathway of the free,
For the last time thy waves I view
Before me roll disdainfully,
Brilliantly beautiful and blue.

Why vain regret? Wherever now
My heedless course I may pursue
One object on thy desert brow
I everlastingly shall view –

A rock, the sepulchre of Fame!
The poor remains of greatness gone

A cold remembrance there became,
There perished great Napoleon.

In torment dire to sleep he lay;
Then, as a tempest echoing rolls,
Another genius whirled away,
Another sovereign of our souls.

He perished. Freedom wept her child,
He left the world his garland bright.
Wail, Ocean, surge in tumult wild,
To sing of thee was his delight.

Impressed upon him was thy mark,
His genius moulded was by thee;
Like thee, he was unfathomed, dark
And untamed in his majesty.

Note: It may interest some to know that Georges d'Anthés was tried by court-martial for his participation in the duel in which Pushkin fell, found guilty, and reduced to the ranks; but, not being a

Russian subject, he was conducted by a gendarme across the frontier and then set at liberty.

Eugene Onйguine

PÉTRI DE VANITÉ, il avait encore plus de cette espèce d'orgueil, qui fait avouer avec la même indifference les bonnes comme les mauvaises actions, suite d'un sentiment de supériorité, peut-être imaginaire. – **Tiré d'une lettre particulière**.

[Note: Written in 1823 at Kishineff and Odessa.]

Canto the First

'The Spleen'

'He rushes at life and exhausts the
passions.'
Prince Viazemski

Canto the First

I

"My uncle's goodness is extreme,
If seriously he hath disease;
He hath acquired the world's esteem

And nothing more important sees;
A paragon of virtue he!
But what a nuisance it will be,
Chained to his bedside night and day
Without a chance to slip away.
Ye need dissimulation base
A dying man with art to soothe,
Beneath his head the pillow smooth,
And physic bring with mournful face,
To sigh and meditate alone:
When will the devil take his own!"

II

Thus mused a madcap young, who drove
Through clouds of dust at postal pace,
By the decree of Mighty Jove,
Inheritor of all his race.
Friends of Liudmila and Ruslan,[1]
Let me present ye to the man,

---

1 Ruslan and Liudmila, the title of Pushkin's first important work, written 1817-20. It is a tale relating the adventures of the knight-errant

Who without more prevarication
The hero is of my narration!
Onéguine, O my gentle readers,
Was born beside the Neva, where
It may be ye were born, or there
Have shone as one of fashion's leaders.
I also wandered there of old,
But cannot stand the northern cold.[2]

III

Having performed his service truly,
Deep into debt his father ran;
Three balls a year he gave ye duly,
At last became a ruined man.
But Eugene was by fate preserved,
For first "madame" his wants observed,
And then "monsieur" supplied her place;[3]

Ruslan in search of his fair lady Liudmila, who has been carried off by a kaldoon, or magician.

2 Written in Bessarabia.

3 In Russia foreign tutors and governesses are commonly styled "monsieur" or "madame."

The boy was wild but full of grace.
"Monsieur l'Abbé" a starving Gaul,
Fearing his pupil to annoy,
Instructed jestingly the boy,
Morality taught scarce at all;
Gently for pranks he would reprove
And in the Summer Garden rove.

IV

When youth's rebellious hour drew near
And my Eugene the path must trace –
The path of hope and tender fear –
Monsieur clean out of doors they chase.
Lo! my Onéguine free as air,
Cropped in the latest style his hair,
Dressed like a London dandy he
The giddy world at last shall see.
He wrote and spoke, so all allowed,
In the French language perfectly,
Danced the mazurka gracefully,
Without the least constraint he bowed.

What more's required? The world replies,
He is a charming youth and wise.

V

We all of us of education
A something somehow have obtained,
Thus, praised be God! a reputation
With us is easily attained.
Onéguine was – so many deemed
[Unerring critics self-esteemed],
Pedantic although scholar like,
In truth he had the happy trick
Without constraint in conversation
Of touching lightly every theme.
Silent, oracular ye'd see him
Amid a serious disputation,
Then suddenly discharge a joke
The ladies' laughter to provoke.

VI

Latin is just now not in vogue,

But if the truth I must relate,
Onéguine knew enough, the rogue
A mild quotation to translate,
A little Juvenal to spout,
With “vale” finish off a note;
Two verses he could recollect
Of the Æneid, but incorrect.
In history he took no pleasure,
The dusty chronicles of earth
For him were but of little worth,
Yet still of anecdotes a treasure
Within his memory there lay,
From Romulus unto our day.

VII

For empty sound the rascal swore he
Existence would not make a curse,
Knew not an iamb from a choree,
Although we read him heaps of verse.
Homer, Theocritus, he jeered,
But Adam Smith to read appeared,
And at economy was great;

That is, he could elucidate
How empires store of wealth unfold,
How flourish, why and wherefore less
If the raw product they possess
The medium is required of gold.
The father scarcely understands
His son and mortgages his lands.

VIII

But upon all that Eugene knew
I have no leisure here to dwell,
But say he was a genius who
In one thing really did excel.
It occupied him from a boy,
A labour, torment, yet a joy,
It whiled his idle hours away
And wholly occupied his day –
The amatory science warm,
Which Ovid once immortalized,
For which the poet agonized
Laid down his life of sun and storm

On the steppes of Moldavia lone,
Far from his Italy – his own.[4]

IX

How soon he learnt deception's art,
Hope to conceal and jealousy,
False confidence or doubt to impart,
Sombre or glad in turn to be,
Haughty appear, subservient,

---

[4] Referring to Tomi, the reputed place of exile of Ovid. Pushkin, then residing in Bessarabia, was in the same predicament as his predecessor in song, though he certainly did not plead guilty to the fact, since he remarks in his ode to Ovid: To exile self-consigned, With self, society, existence, discontent, I visit in these days, with melancholy mind, The country whereunto a mournful age thee sent.

Ovid thus enumerates the causes which brought about his banishment:

"Perdiderint quum me duo crimina, carmen et error, Alterius facti culpa silenda mihi est." Ovidii Nasonis Tristium, lib. ii. 207

Obsequious or indifferent!
What languor would his silence show,
How full of fire his speech would glow!
How artless was the note which spoke
Of love again, and yet again;
How deftly could he transport feign!
How bright and tender was his look,
Modest yet daring! And a tear
Would at the proper time appear.

X

How well he played the greenhorn's part
To cheat the inexperienced fair,
Sometimes by pleasing flattery's art,
Sometimes by ready-made despair;
The feeble moment would espy
Of tender years the modesty
Conquer by passion and address,
Await the long-delayed caress.
Avowal then 'twas time to pray,
Attentive to the heart's first beating,
Follow up love – a secret meeting

Arrange without the least delay –
Then, then – well, in some solitude
Lessons to give he understood!

XI

How soon he learnt to titillate
The heart of the inveterate flirt!
Desirous to annihilate
His own antagonists expert,
How bitterly he would malign,
With many a snare their pathway line!
But ye, O happy husbands, ye
With him were friends eternally:
The crafty spouse caressed him, who
By Faublas in his youth was schooled,[5]
And the suspicious veteran old,
The pompous, swaggering cuckold too,

---

5 Les Aventures du Chevalier de Faublas, a romance of a loose character by Jean Baptiste Louvet de Couvray, b. 1760, d. 1797, famous for his bold oration denouncing Robespierre, Marat and Danton.

Who floats contentedly through life,
Proud of his dinners and his wife!

XII

One morn whilst yet in bed he lay,
His valet brings him letters three.
What, invitations? The same day
As many entertainments be!
A ball here, there a children's treat,
Whither shall my rapscallion flit?
Whither shall he go first? He'll see,
Perchance he will to all the three.
Meantime in matutinal dress
And hat surnamed a "Bolivar"[6]
He hies unto the "Boulevard,"
To loiter there in idleness
Until the sleepless Bréguet chime[7]
Announcing to him dinner-time.

---

6 A la "Bolivar," from the founder of Bolivian independence.

XIII

'Tis dark. He seats him in a sleigh,
"Drive on!" the cheerful cry goes forth,
His furs are powdered on the way
By the fine silver of the north.
He bends his course to Talon's, where[8]
He knows Kaverine will repair.[9]
He enters. High the cork arose
And Comet champagne foaming flows.

---

[7] M. Bréguet, a celebrated Parisian watchmaker – hence a slang term for a watch.

[8] Talon, a famous St. Petersburg restaurateur.

[9] Paul Petròvitch Kaverine, a friend for whom Pushkin in his youth appears to have entertained great respect and admiration. He was an officer in the Hussars of the Guard, and a noted "dandy" and man about town. The poet on one occasion addressed the following impromptu to his friend's portrait:

"Within him daily see the the fires of punch and war,
Upon the fields of Mars a gallant warrior,
A faithful friend to friends, of ladies torturer,
But ever the Hussar."

Before him red roast beef is seen
And truffles, dear to youthful eyes,
Flanked by immortal Strasbourg pies,
The choicest flowers of French cuisine,
And Limburg cheese alive and old
Is seen next pine-apples of gold.

XIV

Still thirst fresh draughts of wine compels
To cool the cutlets' seething grease,
When the sonorous Bréguet tells
Of the commencement of the piece.
A critic of the stage malicious,
A slave of actresses capricious,
Onéguine was a citizen
Of the domains of the side-scene.
To the theatre he repairs
Where each young critic ready stands,
Capers applauds with clap of hands,
With hisses Cleopatra scares,
Moina recalls for this alone
That all may hear his voice's tone.

XV

Thou fairy-land! Where formerly
Shone pungent Satire's dauntless king,
Von Wisine, friend of liberty,
And Kniajnine, apt at copying.
The young Simeonova too there
With Ozeroff was wont to share
Applause, the people's donative.
There our Katènine did revive
Corneille's majestic genius,
Sarcastic Shakhovskoi brought out
His comedies, a noisy rout,
There Didelot became glorious,
There, there, beneath the side-scene's shade
The drama of my youth was played.[10]

---

10 Denis Von Wisine (1741-92), a favourite Russian dramatist. His first comedy "The Brigadier," procured him the favour of the second Catherine. His best, however, is the "Minor" (Niedorosl). Prince Potemkin, after witnessing it, summoned the author, and

XVI

My goddesses, where are your shades?
Do ye not hear my mournful sighs?
Are ye replaced by other maids
Who cannot conjure former joys?
Shall I your chorus hear anew,

---

greeted him with the exclamation, “Die now, Denis!” In fact, his subsequent performances were not of equal merit.

Jacob Borissovitch Kniajnine (1742-91), a clever adapter of French tragedy.

Simeonova, a celebrated tragic actress, who retired from the stage in early life and married a Prince Gagarine.

Ozeroff, one of the best-known Russian dramatists of the period; he possessed more originality than Kniajnine. “Œdipus in Athens,” “Fingal,” “Demetrius Donskoi,” and “Polyxena,” are the best known of his tragedies.

Katènine translated Corneille’s tragedies into Russian.

Didelot, sometime Director of the ballet at the Opera at St. Petersburg.

Russia's Terpsichore review
Again in her ethereal dance?
Or will my melancholy glance
On the dull stage find all things changed,
The disenchanted glass direct
Where I can no more recollect? –
A careless looker-on estranged
In silence shall I sit and yawn
And dream of life's delightful dawn?

XVII

The house is crammed. A thousand
  lamps
On pit, stalls, boxes, brightly blaze,
Impatiently the gallery stamps,
The curtain now they slowly raise.
Obedient to the magic strings,
Brilliant, ethereal, there springs
Forth from the crowd of nymphs
  surrounding
Istomina(*) the nimbly-bounding;
With one foot resting on its tip

Slow circling round its fellow swings
And now she skips and now she springs
Like down from Aeolus's lip,
Now her lithe form she arches o'er
And beats with rapid foot the floor.

[Note: Istomina – A celebrated Circassian dancer of the day, with whom the poet in his extreme youth imagined himself in love.]

XVIII

Shouts of applause! Onéguine passes
Between the stalls, along the toes;
Seated, a curious look with glasses
On unknown female forms he throws.
Free scope he yields unto his glance,
Reviews both dress and countenance,
With all dissatisfaction shows.
To male acquaintances he bows,
And finally he deigns let fall
Upon the stage his weary glance.

He yawns, averts his countenance,
Exclaiming, "We must change 'em all!
I long by ballets have been bored,
Now Didelot scarce can be endured!"

XIX

Snakes, satyrs, loves with many a shout
Across the stage still madly sweep,
Whilst the tired serving-men without
Wrapped in their sheepskins soundly
 sleep.
Still the loud stamping doth not cease,
Still they blow noses, cough, and sneeze,
Still everywhere, without, within,
The lamps illuminating shine;
The steed benumbed still pawing stands
And of the irksome harness tires,
And still the coachmen round the fires[11]

---

[11] In Russia large fires are lighted in winter time in front of the theatres for the benefit of the menials, who, considering the state of the thermometer, cannot be said to have a jovial

Abuse their masters, rub their hands:
But Eugene long hath left the press
To array himself in evening dress.

XX

Faithfully shall I now depict,
Portray the solitary den
Wherein the child of fashion strict
Dressed him, undressed, and dressed
  again?
All that industrial London brings
For tallow, wood and other things
Across the Baltic's salt sea waves,
All which caprice and affluence craves,
All which in Paris eager taste,
Choosing a profitable trade,
For our amusement ever made
And ease and fashionable waste, –

---

time of it. But in this, as in other cases, "habit" alleviates their lot, and they bear the cold with a wonderful equanimity.

Adorned the apartment of Eugene,
Philosopher just turned eighteen.

XXI

China and bronze the tables weight,
Amber on pipes from Stamboul glows,
And, joy of souls effeminate,
Phials of crystal scents enclose.
Combs of all sizes, files of steel,
Scissors both straight and curved as
well,
Of thirty different sorts, lo! brushes
Both for the nails and for the tushes.
Rousseau, I would remark in passing,[12]

[12] "Tout le monde sut qu'il (Grimm) mettait du blanc; et moi, qui n'en croyait rien, je commençai de le croire, non seulement par l'embellissement de son teint, et pour avoir trouvé des tasses de blanc sur la toilette, mais sur ce qu'entrant un matin dans sa chambre, je le trouvais brossant ses ongles avec une petite vergette faite exprès, ouvrage qu'il continua

Could not conceive how serious Grimm
Dared calmly cleanse his nails 'fore him,
Eloquent raver all-surpassing, –
The friend of liberty and laws
In this case quite mistaken was.

XXII

The most industrious man alive
May yet be studious of his nails;
What boots it with the age to strive?
Custom the despot soon prevails.
A new Kaverine Eugene mine,
Dreading the world's remarks malign,
Was that which we are wont to call
A fop, in dress pedantical.
Three mortal hours per diem he
Would loiter by the looking-glass,

---

fièrement devant moi. Je jugeai qu'un homme qui passe deux heures tous les matins à brosser ses ongles peut bien passer quelques instants à remplir de blanc les creux de sa peau."

Confessions de J. J. Rousseau

And from his dressing-room would pass
Like Venus when, capriciously,
The goddess would a masquerade
Attend in male attire arrayed.

XXIII

On this artistical retreat
Having once fixed your interest,
I might to connoisseurs repeat
The style in which my hero dressed;
Though I confess I hardly dare
Describe in detail the affair,
Since words like pantaloons, vest, coat,
To Russ indigenous are not;
And also that my feeble verse –
Pardon I ask for such a sin –
With words of foreign origin
Too much I'm given to intersperse,
Though to the Academy I come
And oft its Dictionary thumb.[13]

---

[13] Refers to Dictionary of the Academy, compiled during the reign of Catherine II under

XXIV

But such is not my project now,
So let us to the ball-room haste,
Whither at headlong speed doth go
Eugene in hackney carriage placed.
Past darkened windows and long streets
Of slumbering citizens he fleets,
Till carriage lamps, a double row,
Cast a gay lustre on the snow,
Which shines with iridescent hues.
He nears a spacious mansion's gate,
By many a lamp illuminate,
And through the lofty windows views
Profiles of lovely dames he knows
And also fashionable beaux.

XXV

Our hero stops and doth alight,
Flies past the porter to the stair,

---

the supervision of Lomonossoff.

But, ere he mounts the marble flight,
With hurried hand smooths down his
 hair.
He enters: in the hall a crowd,
No more the music thunders loud,
Some a mazurka occupies,
Crushing and a confusing noise;
Spurs of the Cavalier Guard clash,
The feet of graceful ladies fly,
And following them ye might espy
Full many a glance like lightning flash,
And by the fiddle's rushing sound
The voice of jealousy is drowned.

XXVI

In my young days of wild delight
On balls I madly used to dote,
Fond declarations they invite
Or the delivery of a note.
So hearken, every worthy spouse,
I would your vigilance arouse,
Attentive be unto my rhymes

And due precautions take betimes.
Ye mothers also, caution use,
Upon your daughters keep an eye,
Employ your glasses constantly,
For otherwise – God only knows!
I lift a warning voice because
I long have ceased to offend the laws.

XXVII

Alas! life's hours which swiftly fly
I've wasted in amusements vain,
But were it not immoral I
Should dearly like a dance again.
I love its furious delight,
The crowd and merriment and light,
The ladies, their fantastic dress,
Also their feet – yet ne'ertheless
Scarcely in Russia can ye find
Three pairs of handsome female feet;
Ah! I still struggle to forget
A pair; though desolate my mind,

Their memory lingers still and seems
To agitate me in my dreams.

XXVIII

When, where, and in what desert land,
Madman, wilt thou from memory raze
Those feet? Alas! on what far strand
Do ye of spring the blossoms graze?
Lapped in your Eastern luxury,
No trace ye left in passing by
Upon the dreary northern snows,
But better loved the soft repose
Of splendid carpets richly wrought.
I once forgot for your sweet cause
The thirst for fame and man's applause,
My country and an exile's lot;
My joy in youth was fleeting e'en
As your light footprints on the green.

XXIX

Diana's bosom, Flora's cheeks,

Are admirable, my dear friend,
But yet Terpsichore bespeaks
Charms more enduring in the end.
For promises her feet reveal
Of untold gain she must conceal,
Their privileged allurements fire
A hidden train of wild desire.
I love them, O my dear Elvine,[14]
Beneath the table-cloth of white,
In winter on the fender bright,
In springtime on the meadows green,
Upon the ball-room's glassy floor
Or by the ocean's rocky shore.

XXX

Beside the stormy sea one day

---

14 Elvine, or Elvina, was not improbably the owner of the seductive feet apostrophized by the poet, since, in 1816, he wrote an ode, "To Her," which commences thus:

"Elvina, my dear, come, give me thine hand," and so forth.

I envied sore the billows tall,
Which rushed in eager dense array
Enamoured at her feet to fall.
How like the billow I desired
To kiss the feet which I admired!
No, never in the early blaze
Of fiery youth's untutored days
So ardently did I desire
A young Armida's lips to press,
Her cheek of rosy loveliness
Or bosom full of languid fire, –
A gust of passion never tore
My spirit with such pangs before.

XXXI

Another time, so willed it Fate,
Immersed in secret thought I stand
And grasp a stirrup fortunate –
Her foot was in my other hand.
Again imagination blazed,
The contact of the foot I raised
Rekindled in my withered heart

The fires of passion and its smart –
Away! and cease to ring their praise
For ever with thy tattling lyre,
The proud ones are not worth the fire
Of passion they so often raise.
The words and looks of charmers sweet
Are oft deceptive – like their feet.

XXXII

Where is Onéguine? Half asleep,
Straight from the ball to bed he goes,
Whilst Petersburg from slumber deep
The drum already doth arouse.
The shopman and the pedlar rise
And to the Bourse the cabman plies;
The Okhtenka with pitcher speeds,[15]
Crunching the morning snow she treads;
Morning awakes with joyous sound;

---

15 i.e. the milkmaid from the Okhta villages, a suburb of St. Petersburg on the right bank of the Neva chiefly inhabited by the labouring classes.

The shutters open; to the skies
In column blue the smoke doth rise;
The German baker looks around
His shop, a night-cap on his head,
And pauses oft to serve out bread.

XXXIII

But turning morning into night,
Tired by the ball’s incessant noise,
The votary of vain delight
Sleep in the shadowy couch enjoys,
Late in the afternoon to rise,
When the same life before him lies
Till morn – life uniform but gay,
To-morrow just like yesterday.
But was our friend Eugene content,
Free, in the blossom of his spring,
Amidst successes flattering
And pleasure’s daily blandishment,
Or vainly ’mid luxurious fare
Was he in health and void of care? –

XXXIV

Even so! His passions soon abated,
Hateful the hollow world became,
Nor long his mind was agitated
By love's inevitable flame.
For treachery had done its worst;
Friendship and friends he likewise curst,
Because he could not gourmandise
Daily beefsteaks and Strasbourg pies
And irrigate them with champagne;
Nor slander viciously could spread
Whene'er he had an aching head;
And, though a plucky scatterbrain,
He finally lost all delight
In bullets, sabres, and in fight.

XXXV

His malady, whose cause I ween
It now to investigate is time,
Was nothing but the British spleen
Transported to our Russian clime.

It gradually possessed his mind;
Though, God be praised! he ne'er
designed
To slay himself with blade or ball,
Indifferent he became to all,
And like Childe Harold gloomily
He to the festival repairs,
Nor boston nor the world's affairs
Nor tender glance nor amorous sigh
Impressed him in the least degree, –
Callous to all he seemed to be.

XXXVI

Ye miracles of courtly grace,
He left **you** first, and I must own
The manners of the highest class
Have latterly vexatious grown;
And though perchance a lady may
Discourse of Bentham or of Say,
Yet as a rule their talk I call
Harmless, but quite nonsensical.
Then they're so innocent of vice,

So full of piety, correct,
So prudent, and so circumspect
Stately, devoid of prejudice,
So inaccessible to men,
Their looks alone produce the spleen.[16]

---

[16] Apropos of this somewhat ungallant sentiment, a Russian scholiast remarks: – "The whole of this ironical stanza is but a refined eulogy of the excellent qualities of our countrywomen. Thus Boileau, in the guise of invective, eulogizes Louis XIV. Russian ladies unite in their persons great acquirements, combined with amiability and strict morality; also a species of Oriental charm which so much captivated Madame de Stael." It will occur to most that the apologist of the Russian fair "doth protest too much." The poet in all probability wrote the offending stanza in a fit of Byronic "spleen," as he would most likely himself have called it. Indeed, since Byron, poets of his school seem to assume this virtue if they have it not, and we take their utterances under its influence for what they are worth.

XXXVII

And you, my youthful damsels fair,
Whom latterly one often meets
Urging your droshkies swift as air
Along Saint Petersburg's paved streets,
From you too Eugene took to flight,
Abandoning insane delight,
And isolated from all men,
Yawning betook him to a pen.
He thought to write, but labour long
Inspired him with disgust and so
Nought from his pen did ever flow,
And thus he never fell among
That vicious set whom I don't blame –
Because a member I became.

XXXVIII

Once more to idleness consigned,
He felt the laudable desire
From mere vacuity of mind
The wit of others to acquire.

A case of books he doth obtain –
He reads at random, reads in vain.
This nonsense, that dishonest seems,
This wicked, that absurd he deems,
All are constrained and fetters bear,
Antiquity no pleasure gave,
The moderns of the ancients rave –
Books he abandoned like the fair,
His book-shelf instantly doth drape
With taffety instead of crape.

XXXIX

Having abjured the haunts of men,
Like him renouncing vanity,
His friendship I acquired just then;
His character attracted me.
An innate love of meditation,
Original imagination,
And cool sagacious mind he had:
I was incensed and he was sad.
Both were of passion satiate
And both of dull existence tired,

Extinct the flame which once had fired;
Both were expectant of the hate
With which blind Fortune oft betrays
The very morning of our days.

XL

He who hath lived and living, thinks,
Must e'en despise his kind at last;
He who hath suffered ofttimes shrinks
From shades of the relentless past.
No fond illusions live to soothe,
But memory like a serpent's tooth
With late repentance gnaws and stings.
All this in many cases brings
A charm with it in conversation.
Onéguine's speeches I abhorred
At first, but soon became inured
To the sarcastic observation,
To witticisms and taunts half-vicious
And gloomy epigrams malicious.

XLI

How oft, when on a summer night
Transparent o'er the Neva beamed
The firmament in mellow light,
And when the watery mirror gleamed
No more with pale Diana's rays,[17]
We called to mind our youthful days –
The days of love and of romance!
Then would we muse as in a trance,
Impressionable for an hour,
And breathe the balmy breath of night;
And like the prisoner's our delight
Who for the greenwood quits his tower,
As on the rapid wings of thought
The early days of life we sought.

XLII

Absorbed in melancholy mood
And o'er the granite coping bent,

---

[17] The midsummer nights in the latitude of St. Petersburg are a prolonged twilight.

Onéguine meditative stood,
E'en as the poet says he leant.[18]
'Tis silent all! Alone the cries
Of the night sentinels arise
And from the Millionaya afar[19]
The sudden rattling of a car.
Lo! on the sleeping river borne,
A boat with splashing oar floats by,
And now we hear delightedly
A jolly song and distant horn;
But sweeter in a midnight dream
Torquato Tasso's strains I deem.

XLIII

Ye billows of blue Hadria's sea,
O Brenta, once more we shall meet

---

[18] Refers to Mouravieff's "Goddess of the Neva." At St. Petersburg the banks of the Neva are lined throughout with splendid granite quays.

[19] A street running parallel to the Neva, and leading from the Winter Palace to the Summer Palace and Garden.

And, inspiration firing me,
Your magic voices I shall greet,
Whose tones Apollo's sons inspire,
And after Albion's proud lyre[20]
Possess my love and sympathy.
The nights of golden Italy
I'll pass beneath the firmament,
Hid in the gondola's dark shade,
Alone with my Venetian maid,
Now talkative, now reticent;
From her my lips shall learn the tongue
Of love which whilom Petrarch sung.

---

20 The strong influence exercised by Byron's genius on the imagination of Pushkin is well known. Shakespeare and other English dramatists had also their share in influencing his mind, which, at all events in its earlier developments, was of an essentially imitative type. As an example of his Shakespearian tastes, see his poem of "Angelo," founded upon "Measure for Measure."

XLIV

When will my hour of freedom come!
Time, I invoke thee! favouring gales
Awaiting on the shore I roam
And beckon to the passing sails.
Upon the highway of the sea
When shall I wing my passage free
On waves by tempests curdled o'er!
'Tis time to quit this weary shore
So uncongenial to my mind,
To dream upon the sunny strand
Of Africa, ancestral land,[21]

---

[21] The poet was, on his mother's side, of African extraction, a circumstance which perhaps accounts for the southern fervour of his imagination. His great-grandfather, Abraham Petròvitch Hannibal, was seized on the coast of Africa when eight years of age by a corsair, and carried a slave to Constantinople. The Russian Ambassador bought and presented him to Peter the Great who caused him to be baptized at Vilnius. Subsequently one of Hannibal's brothers made his way to

Of dreary Russia left behind,
Wherein I felt love's fatal dart,
Wherein I buried left my heart.

XLV

Eugene designed with me to start
And visit many a foreign clime,
But Fortune cast our lots apart
For a protracted space of time.
Just at that time his father died,
And soon Onéguine's door beside
Of creditors a hungry rout
Their claims and explanations shout.
But Eugene, hating litigation
And with his lot in life content,
To a surrender gave consent,
Seeing in this no deprivation,

Constantinople and thence to St. Petersburg for the purpose of ransoming him; but Peter would not surrender his godson who died at the age of ninety-two, having attained the rank of general in the Russian service.

Or counting on his uncle's death
And what the old man might bequeath.

XLVI

And in reality one day
The steward sent a note to tell
How sick to death his uncle lay
And wished to say to him farewell.
Having this mournful document
Perused, Eugene in postchaise went
And hastened to his uncle's side,
But in his heart dissatisfied,
Having for money's sake alone
Sorrow to counterfeit and wail –
Thus we began our little tale –
But, to his uncle's mansion flown,
He found him on the table laid,
A due which must to earth be paid.

XLVII

The courtyard full of serfs he sees,

And from the country all around
Had come both friends and enemies –
Funeral amateurs abound!
The body they consigned to rest,
And then made merry pope and guest,
With serious air then went away
As men who much had done that day.
Lo! my Onéguine rural lord!
Of mines and meadows, woods and
  lakes,
He now a full possession takes,
He who economy abhorred,
Delighted much his former ways
To vary for a few brief days.

XLVIII

For two whole days it seemed a change
To wander through the meadows still,
The cool dark oaken grove to range,
To listen to the rippling rill.
But on the third of grove and mead
He took no more the slightest heed;

They made him feel inclined to doze;
And the conviction soon arose,
Ennui can in the country dwell
Though without palaces and streets,
Cards, balls, routs, poetry or fêtes;
On him spleen mounted sentinel
And like his shadow dogged his life,
Or better, – like a faithful wife.

XLIX

I was for calm existence made,
For rural solitude and dreams,
My lyre sings sweeter in the shade
And more imagination teems.
On innocent delights I dote,
Upon my lake I love to float,
For law I **far niente** take
And every morning I awake
The child of sloth and liberty.
I slumber much, a little read,
Of fleeting glory take no heed.
In former years thus did not I

In idleness and tranquil joy
The happiest days of life employ?

L

Love, flowers, the country, idleness
And fields my joys have ever been;
I like the difference to express
Between myself and my Eugene,
Lest the malicious reader or
Some one or other editor
Of keen sarcastic intellect
Herein my portrait should detect,
And impiously should declare,
To sketch myself that I have tried
Like Byron, bard of scorn and pride,
As if impossible it were
To write of any other elf
Than one's own fascinating self.

LI

Here I remark all poets are

Love to idealize inclined;
I have dreamed many a vision fair
And the recesses of my mind
Retained the image, though short-lived,
Which afterwards the muse revived.
Thus carelessly I once portrayed
Mine own ideal, the mountain maid,
The captives of the Salguir's shore.[22]
But now a question in this wise
Oft upon friendly lips doth rise:
Whom doth thy plaintive Muse adore?
To whom amongst the jealous throng
Of maids dost thou inscribe thy song?

LII

Whose glance reflecting inspiration
With tenderness hath recognized

---

[22] Refers to two of the most interesting productions of the poet. The former line indicates the Prisoner of the Caucasus, the latter, The Fountain of Baktchiserai. The Salguir is a river of the Crimea.

Thy meditative incantation –
Whom hath thy strain immortalized?
None, be my witness Heaven above!
The malady of hopeless love
I have endured without respite.
Happy who thereto can unite
Poetic transport. They impart
A double force unto their song
Who following Petrarch move along
And ease the tortures of the heart –
Perchance they laurels also cull –
But I, in love, was mute and dull.

LIII

The Muse appeared, when love passed
  by
And my dark soul to light was brought;
Free, I renewed the idolatry
Of harmony enshrining thought.
I write, and anguish flies away,
Nor doth my absent pen portray
Around my stanzas incomplete

Young ladies' faces and their feet.
Extinguished ashes do not blaze –
I mourn, but tears I cannot shed –
Soon, of the tempest which hath fled
Time will the ravages efface –
When that time comes, a poem I'll strive
To write in cantos twenty-five.

LIV

I've thought well o'er the general plan,
The hero's name too in advance,
Meantime I'll finish whilst I can
Canto the First of this romance.
I've scanned it with a jealous eye,
Discovered much absurdity,
But will not modify a tittle –
I owe the censorship a little.
For journalistic deglutition
I yield the fruit of work severe.
Go, on the Neva's bank appear,
My very latest composition!

Enjoy the meed which Fame bestows –
Misunderstanding, words and blows.

END OF CANTO THE FIRST

Canto the Second

The Poet

“O Rus!” – Horace

Canto The Second

[Note: Odessa, December 1823.]

I

The village wherein yawned Eugene
Was a delightful little spot,
There friends of pure delight had been
Grateful to Heaven for their lot.
The lonely mansion-house to screen
From gales a hill behind was seen;
Before it ran a stream. Behold!
Afar, where clothed in green and gold
Meadows and cornfields are displayed,
Villages in the distance show
And herds of oxen wandering low;
Whilst nearer, sunk in deeper shade,
A thick immense neglected grove
Extended – haunt which Dryads love.

II

’Twas built, the venerable pile,
As lordly mansions ought to be,
In solid, unpretentious style,
The style of wise antiquity.

Lofty the chambers one and all,
Silk tapestry upon the wall,
Imperial portraits hang around
And stoves of various shapes abound.
All this I know is out of date,
I cannot tell the reason why,
But Eugene, incontestably,
The matter did not agitate,
Because he yawned at the bare view
Of drawing-rooms or old or new.

III

He took the room wherein the old
Man – forty years long in this wise –
His housekeeper was wont to scold,
Look through the window and kill flies.
'Twas plain – an oaken floor ye scan,
Two cupboards, table, soft divan,
And not a speck of dirt descried.
Onéguine oped the cupboards wide.
In one he doth accounts behold,
Here bottles stand in close array,

There jars of cider block the way,
An almanac but eight years old.
His uncle, busy man indeed,
No other book had time to read.

IV

Alone amid possessions great,
Eugene at first began to dream,
If but to lighten Time's dull rate,
Of many an economic scheme;
This anchorite amid his waste
The ancient **barshtchina** replaced
By an **obrok's** indulgent rate:[23]
The peasant blessed his happy fate.
But this a heinous crime appeared
Unto his neighbour, man of thrift,
Who secretly denounced the gift,
And many another slily sneered;

[23] The barshtchina was the corvée, or forced labour of three days per week rendered previous to the emancipation of 1861 by the serfs to their lord.

And all with one accord agreed,
He was a dangerous fool indeed.

[The **obrok** was a species of poll-tax paid by a serf, either in lieu of the forced labour or in consideration of being permitted to exercise a trade or profession elsewhere. Very heavy obroks have at times been levied on serfs possessed of skill or accomplishments, or who had amassed wealth; and circumstances may be easily imagined which, under such a system, might lead to great abuses.]

V

All visited him at first, of course;
But since to the backdoor they led
Most usually a Cossack horse
Upon the Don's broad pastures bred

If they but heard domestic loads
Come rumbling up the neighbouring
  roads,
Most by this circumstance offended
All overtures of friendship ended.
"Oh! what a fool our neighbour is!
He's a freemason, so we think.
Alone he doth his claret drink,
A lady's hand doth never kiss.
'Tis **yes! no!** never **madam! sir!**"[24]
This was his social character.

VI

Into the district then to boot
A new proprietor arrived,
From whose analysis minute
The neighbourhood fresh sport derived.

---

[24] The neighbours complained of Onéguine's want of courtesy. He always replied "da" or "nyet," yes or no, instead of "das" or "nyets" – the final s being a contraction of "sudar" or "sudarinia," i.e. sir or madam.

Vladimir Lenski was his name,
From Gottingen inspired he came,
A worshipper of Kant, a bard,
A young and handsome galliard.
He brought from mystic Germany
The fruits of learning and combined
A fiery and eccentric mind,
Idolatry of liberty,
A wild enthusiastic tongue,
Black curls which to his shoulders hung.

VII

The pervert world with icy chill
Had not yet withered his young breast.
His heart reciprocated still
When Friendship smiled or Love
  caressed.
He was a dear delightful fool –
A nursling yet for Hope to school.
The riot of the world and glare
Still sovereigns of his spirit were,
And by a sweet delusion he

Would soothe the doubtings of his soul,
He deemed of human life the goal
To be a charming mystery:
He racked his brains to find its clue
And marvels deemed he thus should
view.

VIII

This he believed: a kindred spirit
Impelled to union with his own
Lay languishing both day and night –
Waiting his coming – his alone!
He deemed his friends but longed to
make
Great sacrifices for his sake!
That a friend's arm in every case
Felled a calumniator base!
That chosen heroes consecrate,
Friends of the sons of every land,
Exist – that their immortal band
Shall surely, be it soon or late,

Pour on this orb a dazzling light
And bless mankind with full delight.

IX

Compassion now or wrath inspires
And now philanthropy his soul,
And now his youthful heart desires
The path which leads to glory's goal.
His harp beneath that sky had rung
Where sometime Goethe, Schiller sung,
And at the altar of their fame
He kindled his poetic flame.
But from the Muses' loftiest height
The gifted songster never swerved,
But proudly in his song preserved
An ever transcendental flight;
His transports were quite maidenly,
Charming with grave simplicity.

X

He sang of love – to love a slave.

His ditties were as pure and bright
As thoughts which gentle maidens have,
As a babe's slumber, or the light
Of the moon in the tranquil skies,
Goddess of lovers' tender sighs.
He sang of separation grim,
Of what not, and of distant dim,
Of roses to romancers dear;
To foreign lands he would allude,
Where long time he in solitude
Had let fall many a bitter tear:
He sang of life's fresh colours stained
Before he eighteen years attained.

XI

Since Eugene in that solitude
Gifts such as these alone could prize,
A scant attendance Lenski showed
At neighbouring hospitalities.
He shunned those parties boisterous;
The conversation tedious
About the crop of hay, the wine,

The kennel or a kindred line,
Was certainly not erudite
Nor sparkled with poetic fire,
Nor wit, nor did the same inspire
A sense of social delight,
But still more stupid did appear
The gossip of their ladies fair.

XII

Handsome and rich, the neighbourhood
Lenski as a good match received, –
Such is the country custom good;
All mothers their sweet girls believed
Suitable for this semi-Russian.
He enters: rapidly discussion
Shifts, tacks about, until they prate
The sorrows of a single state.
Perchance where Dunia pours out tea
The young proprietor we find;
To Dunia then they whisper: Mind!
And a guitar produced we see,

And Heavens! warbled forth we hear:
Come to my golden palace, dear![25]

XIII

But Lenski, having no desire
Vows matrimonial to break,
With our Onéguine doth aspire
Acquaintance instantly to make.
They met. Earth, water, prose and verse,
Or ice and flame, are not diverse
If they were similar in aught.
At first such contradictions wrought
Mutual repulsion and ennui,
But grown familiar side by side
On horseback every day they ride –
Inseparable soon they be.
Thus oft – this I myself confess –
Men become friends from idleness.

---

25 From the lay of the Russalka, i.e. mermaid of the Dnieper.

XIV

But even thus not now-a-days!
In spite of common sense we're wont
As cyphers others to appraise,
Ourselves as unities to count;
And like Napoleons each of us
A million bipeds reckons thus
One instrument for his own use –
Feeling is silly, dangerous.
Eugene, more tolerant than this
(Though certainly mankind he knew
And usually despised it too),
Exceptionless as no rule is,
A few of different temper deemed,
Feeling in others much esteemed.

XV

With smiling face he Lenski hears;
The poet's fervid conversation
And judgment which unsteady veers
And eye which gleams with inspiration –

All this was novel to Eugene.
The cold reply with gloomy mien
He oft upon his lips would curb,
Thinking: 'tis foolish to disturb
This evanescent boyish bliss.
Time without me will lessons give,
So meantime let him joyous live
And deem the world perfection is!
Forgive the fever youth inspires,
And youthful madness, youthful fires.

XVI

The gulf between them was so vast,
Debate commanded ample food –
The laws of generations past,
The fruits of science, evil, good,
The prejudices all men have,
The fatal secrets of the grave,
And life and fate in turn selected
Were to analysis subjected.
The fervid poet would recite,
Carried away by ecstasy,

Fragments of northern poetry,
Whilst Eugene condescending quite,
Though scarcely following what was
 said,
Attentive listened to the lad.

XVII

But more the passions occupy
The converse of our hermits twain,
And, heaving a regretful sigh,
An exile from their troublous reign,
Eugene would speak regarding these.
Thrice happy who their agonies
Hath suffered but indifferent grown,
Still happier he who ne'er hath known!
By absence who hath chilled his love,
His hate by slander, and who spends
Existence without wife or friends,
Whom jealous transport cannot move,
And who the rent-roll of his race
Ne'er trusted to the treacherous ace.

XVIII

When, wise at length, we seek repose
Beneath the flag of Quietude,
When Passion's fire no longer glows
And when her violence reviewed –
Each gust of temper, silly word,
Seems so unnatural and absurd:
Reduced with effort unto sense,
We hear with interest intense
The accents wild of other's woes,
They stir the heart as heretofore.
So ancient warriors, battles o'er,
A curious interest disclose
In yarns of youthful troopers gay,
Lost in the hamlet far away.

XIX

And in addition youth is flame
And cannot anything conceal,
Is ever ready to proclaim
The love, hate, sorrow, joy, we feel.

Deeming himself a veteran scarred
In love's campaigns Onéguine heard
With quite a lachrymose expression
The youthful poet's fond confession.
He with an innocence extreme
His inner consciousness laid bare,
And Eugene soon discovered there
The story of his young love's dream,
Where plentifully feelings flow
Which we experienced long ago.

XX

Alas! he loved as in our times
Men love no more, as only the
Mad spirit of the man who rhymes
Is still condemned in love to be;
One image occupied his mind,
Constant affection intertwined
And an habitual sense of pain;
And distance interposed in vain,
Nor years of separation all
Nor homage which the Muse demands

Nor beauties of far distant lands
Nor study, banquet, rout nor ball
His constant soul could ever tire,
Which glowed with virginal desire.

XXI

When but a boy he Olga loved
Unknown as yet the aching heart,
He witnessed tenderly and moved
Her girlish gaiety and sport.
Beneath the sheltering oak tree's shade
He with his little maiden played,
Whilst the fond parents, friends thro' life,
Dreamed in the future man and wife.
And full of innocent delight,
As in a thicket's humble shade,
Beneath her parents' eyes the maid
Grew like a lily pure and white,
Unseen in thick and tangled grass
By bee and butterfly which pass.

XXII

'Twas she who first within his breast
Poetic transport did infuse,
And thoughts of Olga first impressed
A mournful temper on his Muse.
Farewell! thou golden days of love!
'Twas then he loved the tangled grove
And solitude and calm delight,
The moon, the stars, and shining night –
The moon, the lamp of heaven above,
To whom we used to consecrate
A promenade in twilight late
With tears which secret sufferers love –
But now in her effulgence pale
A substitute for lamps we hail!

XXIII

Obedient she had ever been
And modest, cheerful as the morn,
As a poetic life serene,
Sweet as the kiss of lovers sworn.

Her eyes were of cerulean blue,
Her locks were of a golden hue,
Her movements, voice and figure slight,
All about Olga – to a light
Romance of love I pray refer,
You'll find her portrait there, I vouch;
I formerly admired her much
But finally grew bored by her.
But with her elder sister I
Must now my stanzas occupy.

XXIV

Tattiana was her appellation.
We are the first who such a name
In pages of a love narration
With such a perversity proclaim.
But wherefore not? – 'Tis pleasant, nice,
Euphonious, though I know a spice
It carries of antiquity
And of the attic. Honestly,
We must admit but little taste

Doth in us or our names appear[26]
(I speak not of our poems here),
And education runs to waste,
Endowing us from out her store
With affectation, – nothing more.

XXV

And so Tattiana was her name,
Nor by her sister's brilliancy
Nor by her beauty she became
The cynosure of every eye.
Shy, silent did the maid appear
As in the timid forest deer,
Even beneath her parents' roof
Stood as estranged from all aloof,
Nearest and dearest knew not how
To fawn upon and love express;
A child devoid of childishness

---

[26] The Russian annotator remarks: "The most euphonious Greek names, e.g. Agathon, Philotas, Theodora, Thekla, etc., are used amongst us by the lower classes only."

To romp and play she ne'er would go:
Oft staring through the window pane
Would she in silence long remain.

XXVI

Contemplativeness, her delight,
E'en from her cradle's earliest dream,
Adorned with many a vision bright
Of rural life the sluggish stream;
Ne'er touched her fingers indolent
The needle nor, o'er framework bent,
Would she the canvas tight enrich
With gay design and silken stitch.
Desire to rule ye may observe
When the obedient doll in sport
An infant maiden doth exhort
Polite demeanour to preserve,
Gravely repeating to another
Recent instructions of its mother.

XXVII

But Tania ne'er displayed a passion
For dolls, e'en from her earliest years,
And gossip of the town and fashion
She ne'er repeated unto hers.
Strange unto her each childish game,
But when the winter season came
And dark and drear the evenings were,
Terrible tales she loved to hear.
And when for Olga nurse arrayed
In the broad meadow a gay rout,
All the young people round about,
At prisoner's base she never played.
Their noisy laugh her soul annoyed,
Their giddy sports she ne'er enjoyed.

XXVIII

She loved upon the balcony
To anticipate the break of day,
When on the pallid eastern sky
The starry beacons fade away,

The horizon luminous doth grow,
Morning's forerunners, breezes blow
And gradually day unfolds.
In winter, when Night longer holds
A hemisphere beneath her sway,
Longer the East inert reclines
Beneath the moon which dimly shines,
And calmly sleeps the hours away,
At the same hour she oped her eyes
And would by candlelight arise.

XXIX

Romances pleased her from the first,
Her all in all did constitute;
In love adventures she was versed,
Rousseau and Richardson to boot.
Not a bad fellow was her father
Though superannuated rather;
In books he saw nought to condemn
But, as he never opened them,
Viewed them with not a little scorn,
And gave himself but little pain

His daughter's book to ascertain
Which 'neath her pillow lay till morn.
His wife was also mad upon
The works of Mr. Richardson.

XXX

She was thus fond of Richardson
Not that she had his works perused,
Or that adoring Grandison
That rascal Lovelace she abused;
But that Princess Pauline of old,
Her Moscow cousin, often told
The tale of these romantic men;
Her husband was a bridegroom then,
And she despite herself would waste
Sighs on another than her lord
Whose qualities appeared to afford
More satisfaction to her taste.
Her Grandison was in the Guard,
A noted fop who gambled hard.

XXXI

Like his, her dress was always nice,
The height of fashion, fitting tight,
But contrary to her advice
The girl in marriage they unite.
Then, her distraction to allay,
The bridegroom sage without delay
Removed her to his country seat,
Where God alone knows whom she met.
She struggled hard at first thus pent,
Night separated from her spouse,
Then became busy with the house,
First reconciled and then content;
Habit was given us in distress
By Heaven in lieu of happiness.

XXXII

Habit alleviates the grief
Inseparable from our lot;
This great discovery relief
And consolation soon begot.

And then she soon 'twixt work and leisure
Found out the secret how at pleasure
To dominate her worthy lord,
And harmony was soon restored.
The workpeople she superintended,
Mushrooms for winter salted down,
Kept the accounts, shaved many a crown,
The bath on Saturdays attended,
When angry beat her maids, I grieve,
And all without her husband's leave.

[Note: The serfs destined for military service used to have
a portion of their heads shaved as a distinctive mark.]

XXXIII

In her friends' albums, time had been,
With blood instead of ink she scrawled,
Baptized Prascovia Pauline,

And in her conversation drawled.
She wore her corset tightly bound,
The Russian N with nasal sound
She would pronounce **à la Française**;
But soon she altered all her ways,
Corset and album and Pauline,
Her sentimental verses all,
She soon forgot, began to call
Akulka who was once Celine,
And had with waddling in the end
Her caps and night-dresses to mend.

XXXIV

As for her spouse he loved her dearly,
In her affairs ne'er interfered,
Entrusted all to her sincerely,
In dressing-gown at meals appeared.
Existence calmly sped along,
And oft at eventide a throng
Of friends unceremonious would
Assemble from the neighbourhood:
They growl a bit – they scandalise –

They crack a feeble joke and smile –
Thus the time passes and meanwhile
Olga the tea must supervise –
'Tis time for supper, now for bed,
And soon the friendly troop hath fled.

XXXV

They in a peaceful life preserved
Customs by ages sanctified,
Strictly the Carnival observed,
Ate Russian pancakes at Shrovetide,
Twice in the year to fast were bound,
Of whirligigs were very fond,
Of Christmas carols, song and dance;
When people with long countenance
On Trinity Sunday yawned at prayer,
Three tears they dropt with humble mein
Upon a bunch of lovage green;
Kvass needful was to them as air;
On guests their servants used to wait

By rank as settled by the State.[27]

The Russian peasants are childishly fond of whirligigs, which
are also much in vogue during the Carnival.

"Christmas Carols" is not an exact equivalent for the Russian
phrase. "Podbliudni pessni," are literally "dish songs," or
songs used with dishes (of water) during the "sviatki" or Holy
Nights, which extend from Christmas to Twelfth Night, for
purposes of divination. Reference will again be made to this

---

27 The foregoing stanza requires explanation. Russian pancakes or "blinni" are consumed vigorously by the lower orders during the Carnival. At other times it is difficult to procure them, at any rate in the large towns.

superstitious practice, which is not confined to Russia. See Note 52.

"Song and dance," the well-known "khorovod," in which the dance proceeds to vocal music.

"Lovage," the **Levisticum officinalis**, is a hardy plant growing very far north, though an inhabitant of our own kitchen gardens.
The passage containing the reference to the three tears and Trinity Sunday was at first deemed irreligious by the Russian censors, and consequently expunged.

Kvass is of various sorts: there is the common **kvass** of fermented rye used by the peasantry, and the more expensive **kvass** of the restaurants, iced and flavoured with various fruits.

The final two lines refer to the "Tchin," or Russian social
hierarchy. There are fourteen grades in the Tchin assigning
relative rank and precedence to the members of the various
departments of the State, civil, military, naval, court,
scientific and educational. The military and naval grades from
the 14th up to the 7th confer personal nobility only, whilst
above the 7th hereditary rank is acquired. In the remaining
departments, civil or otherwise, personal nobility is only
attained with the 9th grade, hereditary with the 4th.]

XXXVI

Thus age approached, the common doom,

And death before the husband wide
Opened the portals of the tomb
And a new diadem supplied.[28]
Just before dinner-time he slept,
By neighbouring families bewept,
By children and by faithful wife
With deeper woe than others' grief.
He was an honest gentleman,
And where at last his bones repose
The epitaph on marble shows:
Demetrius Larine, sinful man,
Servant of God and brigadier,
Enjoyeth peaceful slumber here.

---

28 A play upon the word "venetz," crown, which also signifies a nimbus or glory, and is the symbol of marriage from the fact of two gilt crowns being held over the heads of the bride and bridegroom during the ceremony. The literal meaning of the passage is therefore: his earthly marriage was dissolved and a heavenly one was contracted.

XXXVII

To his Penates now returned,
Vladimir Lenski visited
His neighbour's lowly tomb and mourned
Above the ashes of the dead.
There long time sad at heart he stayed:
"Poor Yorick," mournfully he said,
"How often in thine arms I lay;
How with thy medal I would play,
The Medal Otchakoff conferred![29]
To me he would his Olga give,
Would whisper: shall I so long live?" –
And by a genuine sorrow stirred,
Lenski his pencil-case took out
And an elegiac poem wrote.

---

29 The fortress of Otchakoff was taken by storm on the 18th December 1788 by a Russian army under Prince Potemkin. Thirty thousand Turks are said to have perished during the assault and ensuing massacre.

XXXVIII

Likewise an epitaph with tears
He writes upon his parents' tomb,
And thus ancestral dust reveres.
Oh! on the fields of life how bloom
Harvests of souls unceasingly
By Providence's dark decree!
They blossom, ripen and they fall
And others rise ephemeral!
Thus our light race grows up and lives,
A moment effervescing stirs,
Then seeks ancestral sepulchres,
The appointed hour arrives, arrives!
And our successors soon shall drive
Us from the world wherein we live.

XXXIX

Meantime, drink deeply of the flow
Of frivolous existence, friends;
Its insignificance I know
And care but little for its ends.

To dreams I long have closed mine eyes,
Yet sometimes banished hopes will rise
And agitate my heart again;
And thus it is 'twould cause me pain
Without the faintest trace to leave
This world. I do not praise desire,
Yet still apparently aspire
My mournful fate in verse to weave,
That like a friendly voice its tone
Rescue me from oblivion.

XL

Perchance some heart 'twill agitate,
And then the stanzas of my theme
Will not, preserved by kindly Fate,
Perish absorbed by Lethe's stream.
Then it may be, O flattering tale,
Some future ignoramus shall
My famous portrait indicate
And cry: he was a poet great!
My gratitude do not disdain,
Admirer of the peaceful Muse,

Whose memory doth not refuse
My light productions to retain,
Whose hands indulgently caress
The bays of age and helplessness.

END OF CANTO THE SECOND.

Canto the Third

The Country Damsel

‘Elle était fille, elle était amoureuse’ –
Malfilatre

Canto The Third

[Note: Odessa and Mikhailovskoe, 1824.]

I

"Whither away? Deuce take the bard!" –
"Good-bye, Onéguine, I must go." –
"I won't detain you; but 'tis hard
To guess how you the eve pull
  through." –
"At Làrina's." – "Hem, that is queer!
Pray is it not a tough affair
Thus to assassinate the eve?" –
"Not at all." – "That I can't conceive!
'Tis something of this sort I deem.
In the first place, say, am I right?
A Russian household simple quite,
Who welcome guests with zeal extreme,
Preserves and an eternal prattle
About the rain and flax and cattle." –

II

"No misery I see in that" –
"Boredom, my friend, behold the ill – "
"Your fashionable world I hate,

Domestic life attracts me still,
Where – " – "What! another eclogue spin?
For God's sake, Lenski, don't begin!
What! really going? 'Tis too bad!
But Lenski, I should be so glad
Would you to me this Phyllis show,
Fair source of every fine idea,
Verses and tears et cetera.
Present me." – "You are joking." – "No." –
"Delighted." – "When?" – "This very night.
They will receive us with delight."

III

Whilst homeward by the nearest route
Our heroes at full gallop sped,
Can we not stealthily make out
What they in conversation said? –
"How now, Onéguine, yawning still?" –
"'Tis habit, Lenski." – "Is your ill
More troublesome than usual?" – "No!

How dark the night is getting though!
Hallo, Andriushka, onward race!
The drive becomes monotonous –
Well! Làrina appears to us
An ancient lady full of grace. –
That bilberry wine, I'm sore afraid,
The deuce with my inside has played."

IV

"Say, of the two which was Tattiana?"
"She who with melancholy face
And silent as the maid Svetlana[30]

---

[30] "Svetlana," a short poem by Joukóvski, upon which his fame mainly rests. Joukóvski was an unblushing plagiarist. Many eminent English poets have been laid under contribution by him, often without going through the form of acknowledging the source of inspiration. Even the poem in question cannot be pronounced entirely original, though its intrinsic beauty is unquestionable. It undoubtedly owes its origin to Burger's poem "Leonora," which has found so many English translators. Not content with

Hard by the window took her place." –
"The younger, you're in love with her!"

---

a single development of Burger's ghastly production the Russian poet has directly paraphrased "Leonora" under its own title, and also written a poem "Liudmila" in imitation of it. The principal outlines of these three poems are as follows: A maiden loses her lover in the wars; she murmurs at Providence and is vainly reproved for such blasphemy by her mother. Providence at length loses patience and sends her lover's spirit, to all appearances as if in the flesh, who induces the unfortunate maiden to elope. Instead of riding to a church or bridal chamber the unpleasant bridegroom resorts to the graveyard and repairs to his own grave, from which he has recently issued to execute his errand. It is a repulsive subject. "Svetlana," however, is more agreeable than its prototype "Leonora," inasmuch as the whole catastrophe turns out a dream brought on by "sorcery," during the "sviatki" or Holy Nights (see Canto V. st. x), and the dreamer awakes to hear the tinkling of her lover's sledge approaching. "Svetlana" has been translated by Sir John Bowring.

"Well!" – "I the elder should prefer,
Were I like you a bard by trade –
In Olga's face no life's displayed.
'Tis a Madonna of Vandyk,
An oval countenance and pink,
Yon silly moon upon the brink
Of the horizon she is like!" –
Vladimir something curtly said
Nor further comment that night made.

V

Meantime Onéguine's apparition
At Làrina's abode produced
Quite a sensation; the position
To all good neighbours' sport conduced.
Endless conjectures all propound
And secretly their views expound.
What jokes and guesses now abound,
A beau is for Tattiana found!
In fact, some people were assured
The wedding-day had been arranged,
But the date subsequently changed

Till proper rings could be procured.
On Lenski's matrimonial fate
They long ago had held debate.

VI

Of course Tattiana was annoyed
By such allusions scandalous,
Yet was her inmost soul o'erjoyed
With satisfaction marvellous,
As in her heart the thought sank home,
I am in love, my hour hath come!
Thus in the earth the seed expands
Obedient to warm Spring's commands.
Long time her young imagination
By indolence and languor fired
The fated nutriment desired;
And long internal agitation
Had filled her youthful breast with gloom,
She waited for – I don't know whom!

VII

The fatal hour had come at last –
She oped her eyes and cried: 'tis he!
Alas! for now before her passed
The same warm vision constantly;
Now all things round about repeat
Ceaselessly to the maiden sweet
His name: the tenderness of home
Tiresome unto her hath become
And the kind-hearted servitors:
Immersed in melancholy thought,
She hears of conversation nought
And hated casual visitors,
Their coming which no man expects,
And stay whose length none recollects.

VIII

Now with what eager interest
She the delicious novel reads,
With what avidity and zest
She drinks in those seductive deeds!

All the creations which below
From happy inspiration flow,
The swain of Julia Wolmar,
Malek Adel and De Linar,[31]
Werther, rebellious martyr bold,
And that unrivalled paragon,

---

[31] The heroes of two romances much in vogue in Pushkin's time: the former by Madame Cottin, the latter by the famous Madame Krudener. The frequent mention in the course of this poem of romances once enjoying a European celebrity but now consigned to oblivion, will impress the reader with the transitory nature of merely mediocre literary reputation. One has now to search for the very names of most of the popular authors of Pushkin's day and rummage biographical dictionaries for the dates of their births and deaths. Yet the poet's prime was but fifty years ago, and had he lived to a ripe old age he would have been amongst us still. He was four years younger than the late Mr. Thomas Carlyle. The decadence of Richardson's popularity amongst his countrymen is a fact familiar to all.

The sleep-compelling Grandison,
Our tender dreamer had enrolled
A single being: ’twas in fine
No other than Onéguine mine.

IX

Dreaming herself the heroine
Of the romances she preferred,
Clarissa, Julia, Delphine, – [32]
Tattiana through the forest erred,
And the bad book accompanies.
Upon those pages she descries
Her passion’s faithful counterpart,
Fruit of the yearnings of the heart.
She heaves a sigh and deep intent
On raptures, sorrows not her own,
She murmurs in an undertone
A letter for her hero meant:

---

[32] Referring to Richardson’s “Clarissa Harlowe,” “La Nouvelle Heloise,” and Madame de Stael’s “Delphine.”

That hero, though his merit shone,
Was certainly no Grandison.

X

Alas! my friends, the years flit by
And after them at headlong pace
The evanescent fashions fly
In motley and amusing chase.
The world is ever altering!
Farthingales, patches, were the thing,
And courtier, fop, and usurer
Would once in powdered wig appear;
Time was, the poet's tender quill
In hopes of everlasting fame
A finished madrigal would frame
Or couplets more ingenious still;
Time was, a valiant general might
Serve who could neither read nor write.

XI

Time was, in style magniloquent

Authors replete with sacred fire
Their heroes used to represent
All that perfection could desire;
Ever by adverse fate oppressed,
Their idols they were wont to invest
With intellect, a taste refined,
And handsome countenance combined,
A heart wherein pure passion burnt;
The excited hero in a trice
Was ready for self-sacrifice,
And in the final tome we learnt,
Vice had due punishment awarded,
Virtue was with a bride rewarded.

XII

But now our minds are mystified
And Virtue acts as a narcotic,
Vice in romance is glorified
And triumphs in career erotic.
The monsters of the British Muse
Deprive our schoolgirls of repose,
The idols of their adoration

A Vampire fond of meditation,
Or Melmoth, gloomy wanderer he,
The Eternal Jew or the Corsair
Or the mysterious Sbogar.[33]
Byron's capricious phantasy
Could in romantic mantle drape
E'en hopeless egoism's dark shape.

XIII

My friends, what means this odd
  digression?
May be that I by heaven's decrees
Shall abdicate the bard's profession,
And shall adopt some new caprice.
Thus having braved Apollo's rage
With humble prose I'll fill my page
And a romance in ancient style

---

33 "Melmoth," a romance by Maturin, and "Jean Sbogar," by Ch. Nodier. "The Vampire," a tale published in 1819, was erroneously attributed to Lord Byron. "Salathiel; the Eternal Jew," a romance by Geo. Croly.

Shall my declining years beguile;
Nor shall my pen paint terribly
The torment born of crime unseen,
But shall depict the touching scene
Of Russian domesticity;
I will descant on love's sweet dream,
The olden time shall be my theme.

XIV

Old people's simple conversations
My unpretending page shall fill,
Their offspring's innocent flirtations
By the old lime-tree or the rill,
Their Jealousy and separation
And tears of reconciliation:
Fresh cause of quarrel then I'll find,
But finally in wedlock bind.
The passionate speeches I'll repeat,
Accents of rapture or despair
I uttered to my lady fair
Long ago, prostrate at her feet.
Then they came easily enow,

My tongue is somewhat rusty now.

XV

Tattiana! sweet Tattiana, see!
What bitter tears with thee I shed!
Thou hast resigned thy destiny
Unto a ruthless tyrant dread.
Thou'lt suffer, dearest, but before,
Hope with her fascinating power
To dire contentment shall give birth
And thou shalt taste the joys of earth.
Thou'lt quaff love's sweet envenomed
  stream,
Fantastic images shall swarm
In thy imagination warm,
Of happy meetings thou shalt dream,
And wheresoe'er thy footsteps err,
Confront thy fated torturer!

XVI

Love's pangs Tattiana agonize.

She seeks the garden in her need –
Sudden she stops, casts down her eyes
And cares not farther to proceed;
Her bosom heaves whilst crimson hues
With sudden flush her cheeks suffuse,
Barely to draw her breath she seems,
Her eye with fire unwonted gleams.
And now 'tis night, the guardian moon
Sails her allotted course on high,
And from the misty woodland nigh
The nightingale trills forth her tune;
Restless Tattiana sleepless lay
And thus unto her nurse did say:

XVII

"Nurse, 'tis so close I cannot rest.
Open the window – sit by me."
"What ails thee, dear?" – "I feel depressed.
Relate some ancient history."
"But which, my dear? – In days of yore
Within my memory I bore
Many an ancient legend which

In monsters and fair dames was rich;
But now my mind is desolate,
What once I knew is clean forgot –
Alas! how wretched now my lot!"
"But tell me, nurse, can you relate
The days which to your youth belong?
Were you in love when you were
  young?" –

XVIII

"Alack! Tattiana," she replied,
"We never loved in days of old,
My mother-in-law who lately died[34]
Had killed me had the like been told."
"How came you then to wed a man?" –
"Why, as God ordered! My Ivan
Was younger than myself, my light,

---

[34] A young married couple amongst Russian peasants reside in the house of the bridegroom's father till the "tiaglo," or family circle is broken up by his death.

For I myself was thirteen quite;[35]
The matchmaker a fortnight sped,
Her suit before my parents pressing:
At last my father gave his blessing,
And bitter tears of fright I shed.
Weeping they loosed my tresses long[36]

---

[35] Marriages amongst Russian serfs used formerly to take place at ridiculously early ages. Haxthausen asserts that strong hearty peasant women were to be seen at work in the fields with their infant husbands in their arms. The inducement lay in the fact that the "tiaglo" (see previous note) received an additional lot of the communal land for every male added to its number, though this could have formed an inducement in the southern and fertile provinces of Russia only, as it is believed that agriculture in the north is so unremunerative that land has often to be forced upon the peasants, in order that the taxes, for which the whole Commune is responsible to Government, may be paid. The abuse of early marriages was regulated by Tsar Nicholas.

[36] Courtships were not unfrequently carried

And led me off to church with song."

XIX

"Then amongst strangers I was left –
But I perceive thou dost not heed – "
"Alas! dear nurse, my heart is cleft,
Mortally sick I am indeed.
Behold, my sobs I scarce restrain – "
"My darling child, thou art in pain. –
The Lord deliver her and save!
Tell me at once what wilt thou have?
I'll sprinkle thee with holy water. –
How thy hands burn!" – "Dear nurse,
  I'm well.
I am – in love – you know – don't tell!"
"The Lord be with thee, O my

---

on in the larger villages, which alone could support such an individual, by means of a "svakha," or matchmaker. In Russia unmarried girls wear their hair in a single long plait or tail, "kossa;" the married women, on the other hand, in two, which are twisted into the head-gear.

daughter!" –
And the old nurse a brief prayer said
And crossed with trembling hand the maid.

XX

"I am in love," her whispers tell
The aged woman in her woe:
"My heart's delight, thou art not well." –
"I am in love, nurse! leave me now."
Behold! the moon was shining bright
And showed with an uncertain light
Tattiana's beauty, pale with care,
Her tears and her dishevelled hair;
And on the footstool sitting down
Beside our youthful heroine fair,
A kerchief round her silver hair
The aged nurse in ample gown,[37]

---

[37] It is thus that I am compelled to render a female garment not known, so far as I am aware, to Western Europe. It is called by the natives "doushegreika," that is to say, "warmer

Whilst all creation seemed to dream
Enchanted by the moon's pale beam.

XXI

But borne in spirit far away
Tattiana gazes on the moon,
And starting suddenly doth say:
"Nurse, leave me. I would be alone.
Pen, paper bring: the table too
Draw near. I soon to sleep shall go –
Good-night." Behold! she is alone!
'Tis silent – on her shines the moon –
Upon her elbow she reclines,
And Eugene ever in her soul
Indites an inconsiderate scroll
Wherein love innocently pines.
Now it is ready to be sent –
For whom, Tattiana, is it meant?

---

of the soul" – in French, chaufferette de l'âme. It is a species of thick pelisse worn over the "sarafan," or gown.

XXII

I have known beauties cold and raw
As Winter in their purity,
Striking the intellect with awe
By dull insensibility,
And I admired their common sense
And natural benevolence,
But, I acknowledge, from them fled;
For on their brows I trembling read
The inscription o'er the gates of Hell
"Abandon hope for ever here!"[38]
Love to inspire doth woe appear
To such – delightful to repel.
Perchance upon the Neva e'en
Similar dames ye may have seen.

XXIII

Amid submissive herds of men
Virgins miraculous I see,

---

[38] A Russian annotator complains that the poet has mutilated Dante's famous line.

Who selfishly unmoved remain
Alike by sighs and flattery.
But what astonished do I find
When harsh demeanour hath consigned
A timid love to banishment? –
On fresh allurements they are bent,
At least by show of sympathy;
At least their accents and their words
Appear attuned to softer chords;
And then with blind credulity
The youthful lover once again
Pursues phantasmagoria vain.

XXIV

Why is Tattiana guiltier deemed? –
Because in singleness of thought
She never of deception dreamed
But trusted the ideal she wrought? –
Because her passion wanted art,
Obeyed the impulses of heart? –
Because she was so innocent,
That Heaven her character had blent

With an imagination wild,
With intellect and strong volition
And a determined disposition,
An ardent heart and yet so mild? –
Doth love's incautiousness in her
So irremissible appear?

XXV

O ye whom tender love hath pained
Without the ken of parents both,
Whose hearts responsive have remained
To the impressions of our youth,
The all-entrancing joys of love –
Young ladies, if ye ever strove
The mystic lines to tear away
A lover's letter might convey,
Or into bold hands anxiously
Have e'er a precious tress consigned,
Or even, silent and resigned,
When separation's hour drew nigh,
Have felt love's agitated kiss
With tears, confused emotions, bliss, –

XXVI

With unanimity complete,
Condemn not weak Tattiana mine;
Do not cold-bloodedly repeat
The sneers of critics superfine;
And you, O maids immaculate,
Whom vice, if named, doth agitate
E'en as the presence of a snake,
I the same admonition make.
Who knows? with love's consuming flame
Perchance you also soon may burn,
Then to some gallant in your turn
Will be ascribed by treacherous Fame
The triumph of a conquest new.
The God of Love is after you!

XXVII

A coquette loves by calculation,
Tattiana's love was quite sincere,
A love which knew no limitation,
Even as the love of children dear.

She did not think "procrastination
Enhances love in estimation
And thus secures the prey we seek.
His vanity first let us pique
With hope and then perplexity,
Excruciate the heart and late
With jealous fire resuscitate,
Lest jaded with satiety,
The artful prisoner should seek
Incessantly his chains to break."

XXVIII

I still a complication view,
My country's honour and repute
Demands that I translate for you
The letter which Tattiana wrote.
At Russ she was by no means clever
And read our newspapers scarce ever,
And in her native language she
Possessed nor ease nor fluency,
So she in French herself expressed.
I cannot help it I declare,

Though hitherto a lady ne'er
In Russ her love made manifest,
And never hath our language proud
In correspondence been allowed.[39]

XXIX

They wish that ladies should, I hear,
Learn Russian, but the Lord defend!
I can't conceive a little dear

---

[39] It is well known that until the reign of the late Tsar French was the language of the Russian court and of Russian fashionable society. It should be borne in mind that at the time this poem was written literary warfare more or less open was being waged between two hostile schools of Russian men of letters. These consisted of the Arzamass, or French school, to which Pushkin himself together with his uncle Vassili Pushkin the "Nestor of the Arzamass" belonged, and their opponents who devoted themselves to the cultivation of the vernacular.

With the "Well-Wisher" in her hand![40]
I ask, all ye who poets are,
Is it not true? the objects fair,
To whom ye for unnumbered crimes
Had to compose in secret rhymes,
To whom your hearts were consecrate, –
Did they not all the Russian tongue
With little knowledge and that wrong
In charming fashion mutilate?
Did not their lips with foreign speech
The native Russian tongue impeach?

XXX

God grant I meet not at a ball
Or at a promenade mayhap,
A schoolmaster in yellow shawl
Or a professor in tulle cap.

---

40 The "Blago-Namièrenni," or "Well-Wisher," was an inferior Russian newspaper of the day, much scoffed at by contemporaries. The editor once excused himself for some gross error by pleading that he had been "on the loose."

As rosy lips without a smile,
The Russian language I deem vile
Without grammatical mistakes.
May be, and this my terror wakes,
The fair of the next generation,
As every journal now entreats,
Will teach grammatical conceits,
Introduce verse in conversation.
But I – what is all this to me?
Will to the old times faithful be.

XXXI

Speech careless, incorrect, but soft,
With inexact pronunciation
Raises within my breast as oft
As formerly much agitation.
Repentance wields not now her spell
And gallicisms I love as well
As the sins of my youthful days
Or Bogdanovitch's sweet lays.[41]

[41] Hippolyte Bogdanovitch – b. 1743, d. 1803 – though possessing considerable

But I must now employ my Muse
With the epistle of my fair;
I promised! – Did I so? – Well, there!
Now I am ready to refuse.
I know that Parny's tender pen[42]

---

poetical talent was like many other Russian authors more remarkable for successful imitation than for original genius. His most remarkable production is "Doushenka," "The Darling," a composition somewhat in the style of La Fontaine's "Psyche." Its merit consists in graceful phraseology, and a strong pervading sense of humour.

42 Parny – a French poet of the era of the first Napoleon, b. 1753, d. 1814. Introduced to the aged Voltaire during his last visit to Paris, the patriarch laid his hands upon the youth's head and exclaimed: "Mon cher Tibulle." He is chiefly known for his erotic poetry which attracted the affectionate regard of the youthful Pushkin when a student at the Lyceum. We regret to add that, having accepted a pension from Napoleon, Parny forthwith proceeded to damage his literary reputation by inditing an "epic" poem entitled "Goddam! Goddam! par un French

Is no more cherished amongst men.

XXXII

Bard of the "Feasts," and mournful
breast,[43]
If thou wert sitting by my side,
With this immoderate request
I should alarm our friendship tried:
In one of thine enchanting lays
To russify the foreign phrase
Of my impassioned heroine.

– Dog." It is descriptive of the approaching conquest of Britain by Napoleon, and treats the embryo enterprise as if already conducted to a successful conclusion and become matter of history. A good account of the bard and his creations will be found in the Saturday Review of the 2d August 1879.

[43] Evgeny Baratynski, a contemporary of Pushkin and a lyric poet of some originality and talent. The "Feasts" is a short brilliant poem in praise of conviviality. Pushkin is therein praised as the best of companions "beside the bottle."

Where art thou? Come! pretensions mine
I yield with a low reverence;
But lonely beneath Finnish skies
Where melancholy rocks arise
He wanders in his indolence;
Careless of fame his spirit high
Hears not my importunity!

XXXIII

Tattiana's letter I possess,
I guard it as a holy thing,
And though I read it with distress,
I'm o'er it ever pondering.
Inspired by whom this tenderness,
This gentle daring who could guess?
Who this soft nonsense could impart,
Imprudent prattle of the heart,
Attractive in its banefulness?
I cannot understand. But lo!
A feeble version read below,
A print without the picture's grace,
Or, as it were, the Freischutz' score

Strummed by a timid schoolgirl o'er.
Tattiana's Letter to Onéguine
I write to you! Is more required?
Can lower depths beyond remain?
'Tis in your power now, if desired,
To crush me with a just disdain.
But if my lot unfortunate
You in the least commiserate
You will not all abandon me.
At first, I clung to secrecy:
Believe me, of my present shame
You never would have heard the name,
If the fond hope I could have fanned
At times, if only once a week,
To see you by our fireside stand,
To listen to the words you speak,
Address to you one single phrase
And then to meditate for days
Of one thing till again we met.
'Tis said you are a misanthrope,
In country solitude you mope,
And we – an unattractive set –
Can hearty welcome give alone.

Why did you visit our poor place?
Forgotten in the village lone,
I never should have seen your face
And bitter torment never known.
The untutored spirit's pangs calmed down
By time (who can anticipate?)
I had found my predestinate,
Become a faithful wife and e'en
A fond and careful mother been.

Another! to none other I
My heart's allegiance can resign,
My doom has been pronounced on high,
'Tis Heaven's will and I am thine.
The sum of my existence gone
But promise of our meeting gave,
I feel thou wast by God sent down
My guardian angel to the grave.
Thou didst to me in dreams appear,
Unseen thou wast already dear.
Thine eye subdued me with strange glance,

I heard thy voice's resonance
Long ago. Dream it cannot be!
Scarce hadst thou entered thee I knew,
I flushed up, stupefied I grew,
And cried within myself: 'tis he!
Is it not truth? in tones suppressed
With thee I conversed when I bore
Comfort and succour to the poor,
And when I prayer to Heaven addressed
To ease the anguish of my breast.
Nay! even as this instant fled,
Was it not thou, O vision bright,
That glimmered through the radiant night
And gently hovered o'er my head?
Was it not thou who thus didst stoop
To whisper comfort, love and hope?
Who art thou? Guardian angel sent
Or torturer malevolent?
Doubt and uncertainty decide:
All this may be an empty dream,
Delusions of a mind untried,
Providence otherwise may deem –
Then be it so! My destiny

From henceforth I confide to thee!
Lo! at thy feet my tears I pour
And thy protection I implore.
Imagine! Here alone am I!
No one my anguish comprehends,
At times my reason almost bends,
And silently I here must die –
But I await thee: scarce alive
My heart with but one look revive;
Or to disturb my dreams approach
Alas! with merited reproach.

'Tis finished. Horrible to read!
With shame I shudder and with dread –
But boldly I myself resign:
Thine honour is my countersign!

XXXIV

Tattiana moans and now she sighs
And in her grasp the letter shakes,
Even the rosy wafer dries
Upon her tongue which fever bakes.

Her head upon her breast declines
And an enchanting shoulder shines
From her half-open vest of night.
But lo! already the moon's light
Is waning. Yonder valley deep
Looms gray behind the mist and morn
Silvers the brook; the shepherd's horn
Arouses rustics from their sleep.
'Tis day, the family downstairs,
But nought for this Tattiana cares.

XXXV

The break of day she doth not see,
But sits in bed with air depressed,
Nor on the letter yet hath she
The image of her seal impressed.
But gray Phillippevna the door
Opened with care, and entering bore
A cup of tea upon a tray.
"'Tis time, my child, arise, I pray!
My beauty, thou art ready too.
My morning birdie, yesternight

I was half silly with affright.
But praised be God! in health art thou!
The pains of night have wholly fled,
Thy cheek is as a poppy red!"

XXXVI

"Ah! nurse, a favour do for me!" –
"Command me, darling, what you
choose" –
"Do not – you might – suspicious be;
But look you – ah! do not refuse."
"I call to witness God on high – "
"Then send your grandson quietly
To take this letter to O – Well!
Unto our neighbour. Mind you tell –
Command him not to say a word –
I mean my name not to repeat."
"To whom is it to go, my sweet?
Of late I have been quite absurd, –
So many neighbours here exist –
Am I to go through the whole list?"

XXXVII

"How dull you are this morning, nurse!"
"My darling, growing old am I!
In age the memory gets worse,
But I was sharp in times gone by.
In times gone by thy bare command – "
"Oh! nurse, nurse, you don't understand!
What is thy cleverness to me?
The letter is the thing, you see, –
Onéguine's letter!" – "Ah! the thing!
Now don't be cross with me, my soul,
You know that I am now a fool –
But why are your cheeks whitening?"
"Nothing, good nurse, there's nothing
  wrong,
But send your grandson before long."

XXXVIII

No answer all that day was borne.
Another passed; 'twas just the same.
Pale as a ghost and dressed since morn

Tattiana waits. No answer came!
Olga's admirer came that day:
"Tell me, why doth your comrade stay?"
The hostess doth interrogate:
"He hath neglected us of late." –
Tattiana blushed, her heart beat quick –
"He promised here this day to ride,"
Lenski unto the dame replied,
"The post hath kept him, it is like."
Shamefaced, Tattiana downward looked
As if he cruelly had joked!

XXXIX

'Twas dusk! Upon the table bright
Shrill sang the **samovar** at eve,[44]

---

[44] The *samovar*, i.e. "self-boiler," is merely an urn for hot water having a fire in the center. We may observe a similar contrivance in our own old-fashioned tea-urns which are provided with a receptacle for a red-hot iron cylinder in center. The tea-pot is usually placed on the top of the *samovar*.

The china teapot too ye might
In clouds of steam above perceive.
Into the cups already sped
By Olga's hand distributed
The fragrant tea in darkling stream,
And a boy handed round the cream.
Tania doth by the casement linger
And breathes upon the chilly glass,
Dreaming of what not, pretty lass,
And traces with a slender finger
Upon its damp opacity,
The mystic monogram, O. E.

XL

In the meantime her spirit sinks,
Her weary eyes are filled with tears –
A horse's hoofs she hears – She shrinks!
Nearer they come – Eugene appears!
Ah! than a spectre from the dead
More swift the room Tattiana fled,
From hall to yard and garden flies,
Not daring to cast back her eyes.

She fears and like an arrow rushes
Through park and meadow, wood and
  brake,
The bridge and alley to the lake,
Brambles she snaps and lilacs crushes,
The flowerbeds skirts, the brook doth
  meet,
Till out of breath upon a seat

XLI

She sank. –
"He's here! Eugene is here!
Merciful God, what will he deem?"
Yet still her heart, which torments tear,
Guards fondly hope's uncertain dream.
She waits, on fire her trembling frame –
Will he pursue? – But no one came.
She heard of servant-maids the note,
Who in the orchards gathered fruit,
Singing in chorus all the while.
(This by command; for it was found,
However cherries might abound,

They disappeared by stealth and guile,
So mouths they stopt with song, not
  fruit –
Device of rural minds acute!)
The Maidens' Song

Young maidens, fair maidens,
Friends and companions,
Disport yourselves, maidens,
Arouse yourselves, fair ones.
Come sing we in chorus
The secrets of maidens.
Allure the young gallant
With dance and with song.
As we lure the young gallant,
Espy him approaching,
Disperse yourselves, darlings,
And pelt him with cherries,
With cherries, red currants,
With raspberries, cherries.
Approach not to hearken
To secrets of virgins,

Approach not to gaze at
The frolics of maidens.

XLII

They sang, whilst negligently seated,
Attentive to the echoing sound,
Tattiana with impatience waited
Until her heart less high should bound –
Till the fire in her cheek decreased;
But tremor still her frame possessed,
Nor did her blushes fade away,
More crimson every moment they.
Thus shines the wretched butterfly,
With iridescent wing doth flap
When captured in a schoolboy's cap;
Thus shakes the hare when suddenly
She from the winter corn espies
A sportsman who in covert lies.

XLIII

But finally she heaves a sigh,

And rising from her bench proceeds;
But scarce had turned the corner nigh,
Which to the neighbouring alley leads,
When Eugene like a ghost did rise
Before her straight with roguish eyes.
Tattiana faltered, and became
Scarlet as burnt by inward flame.
But this adventure's consequence
To-day, my friends, at any rate,
I am not strong enough to state;
I, after so much eloquence,
Must take a walk and rest a bit –
Some day I'll somehow finish it.

END OF CANTO THE THIRD

Canto the Fourth

Rural Life

'La Morale est dans la nature des choses.'
– Necker

Canto The Fourth

[Mikhailovskoe, 1825]

Canto the Fourth

I

The less we love a lady fair
The easier 'tis to gain her grace,
And the more surely we ensnare
Her in the pitfalls which we place.
Time was when cold seduction strove
To swagger as the art of love,
Everywhere trumpeting its feats,
Not seeking love but sensual sweets.
But this amusement delicate
Was worthy of that old baboon,
Our fathers used to dote upon;
The Lovelaces are out of date,
Their glory with their heels of red
And long perukes hath vanishèd.

II

For who imposture can endure,
A constant harping on one tune,
Serious endeavours to assure
What everybody long has known;

Ever to hear the same replies
And overcome antipathies
Which never have existed, e'en
In little maidens of thirteen?
And what like menaces fatigues,
Entreaties, oaths, fictitious fear,
Epistles of six sheets or near,
Rings, tears, deceptions and intrigues,
Aunts, mothers and their scrutiny,
And husbands' tedious amity?

III

Such were the musings of Eugene.
He in the early years of life
Had a deluded victim been
Of error and the passions' strife.
By daily life deteriorated,
Awhile this beauty captivated,
And that no longer could inspire.
Slowly exhausted by desire,
Yet satiated with success,
In solitude or worldly din,

He heard his soul's complaint within,
With laughter smothered weariness:
And thus he spent eight years of time,
Destroyed the blossom of his prime.

IV

Though beauty he no more adored,
He still made love in a queer way;
Rebuffed – as quickly reassured,
Jilted – glad of a holiday.
Without enthusiasm he met
The fair, nor parted with regret,
Scarce mindful of their love and guile.
Thus a guest with composure will
To take a hand at whist oft come:
He takes his seat, concludes his game,
And straight returning whence he came,
Tranquilly goes to sleep at home,
And in the morning doth not know
Whither that evening he will go.

V

However, Tania's letter reading,
Eugene was touched with sympathy;
The language of her girlish pleading
Aroused in him sweet reverie.
He called to mind Tattiana's grace,
Pallid and melancholy face,
And in a vision, sinless, bright,
His spirit sank with strange delight.
May be the empire of the sense,
Regained authority awhile,
But he desired not to beguile
Such open-hearted innocence.
But to the garden once again
Wherein we lately left the twain.

VI

Two minutes they in silence spent,
Onéguine then approached and said:
"You have a letter to me sent.
Do not excuse yourself. I read

Confessions which a trusting heart
May well in innocence impart.
Charming is your sincerity,
Feelings which long had ceased to be
It wakens in my breast again.
But I came not to adulate:
Your frankness I shall compensate
By an avowal just as plain.
An ear to my confession lend;
To thy decree my will I bend.

VII

"If the domestic hearth could bless –
My sum of happiness contained;
If wife and children to possess
A happy destiny ordained:
If in the scenes of home I might
E'en for an instant find delight,
Then, I say truly, none but thee
I would desire my bride to be –
I say without poetic phrase,
Found the ideal of my youth,

Thee only would I choose, in truth,
As partner of my mournful days,
Thee only, pledge of all things bright,
And be as happy – as I might.

VIII

"But strange am I to happiness;
'Tis foreign to my cast of thought;
Me your perfections would not bless;
I am not worthy them in aught;
And honestly 'tis my belief
Our union would produce but grief.
Though now my love might be intense,
Habit would bring indifference.
I see you weep. Those tears of yours
Tend not my heart to mitigate,
But merely to exasperate;
Judge then what roses would be ours,
What pleasures Hymen would prepare
For us, may be for many a year.

IX

"What can be drearier than the house,
Wherein the miserable wife
Deplores a most unworthy spouse
And leads a solitary life?
The tiresome man, her value knowing,
Yet curses on his fate bestowing,
Is full of frigid jealousy,
Mute, solemn, frowning gloomily.
Such am I. This did ye expect,
When in simplicity ye wrote
Your innocent and charming note
With so much warmth and intellect?
Hath fate apportioned unto thee
This lot in life with stern decree?

X

"Ideas and time ne'er backward move;
My soul I cannot renovate –
I love you with a brother's love,
Perchance one more affectionate.

Listen to me without disdain.
A maid hath oft, may yet again
Replace the visions fancy drew;
Thus trees in spring their leaves renew
As in their turn the seasons roll.
'Tis evidently Heaven's will
You fall in love again. But still –
Learn to possess more self-control.
Not all will like myself proceed –
And thoughtlessness to woe might lead."

XI

Thus did our friend Onéguine preach:
Tattiana, dim with tears her eyes,
Attentive listened to his speech,
All breathless and without replies.
His arm he offers. Mute and sad
(**Mechanically**, let us add),
Tattiana doth accept his aid;
And, hanging down her head, the maid
Around the garden homeward hies.
Together they returned, nor word

Of censure for the same incurred;
The country hath its liberties
And privileges nice allowed,
Even as Moscow, city proud.

XII

Confess, O ye who this peruse,
Onéguine acted very well
By poor Tattiana in the blues;
'Twas not the first time, I can tell
You, he a noble mind disclosed,
Though some men, evilly disposed,
Spared him not their asperities.
His friends and also enemies
(One and the same thing it may be)
Esteemed him much as the world goes.
Yes! every one must have his foes,
But Lord! from friends deliver me!
The deuce take friends, my friends, amends
I've had to make for having friends!

XIII

But how? Quite so. Though I dismiss
Dark, unavailing reverie,
I just hint, in parenthesis,
There is no stupid calumny
Born of a babbler in a loft
And by the world repeated oft,
There is no fishmarket retort
And no ridiculous report,
Which your true friend with a sweet smile
Where fashionable circles meet
A hundred times will not repeat,
Quite inadvertently meanwhile;
And yet he in your cause would strive
And loves you as – a relative!

XIV

Ahem! Ahem! My reader noble,
Are all your relatives quite well?
Permit me; is it worth the trouble
For your instruction here to tell

What I by relatives conceive?
These are your relatives, believe:
Those whom we ought to love, caress,
With spiritual tenderness;
Whom, as the custom is of men,
We visit about Christmas Day,
Or by a card our homage pay,
That until Christmas comes again
They may forget that we exist.
And so – God bless them, if He list.

XV

In this the love of the fair sex
Beats that of friends and relatives:
In love, although its tempests vex,
Our liberty at least survives:
Agreed! but then the whirl of fashion,
The natural fickleness of passion,
The torrent of opinion,
And the fair sex as light as down!
Besides the hobbies of a spouse
Should be respected throughout life

By every proper-minded wife,
And this the faithful one allows,
When in as instant she is lost, –
Satan will jest, and at love's cost.

XVI

Oh! where bestow our love? Whom
  trust?
Where is he who doth not deceive?
Who words and actions will adjust
To standards in which we believe?
Oh! who is not calumnious?
Who labours hard to humour us?
To whom are our misfortunes grief
And who is not a tiresome thief?
My venerated reader, oh!
Cease the pursuit of shadows vain,
Spare yourself unavailing pain
And all your love on self bestow;
A worthy object 'tis, and well
I know there's none more amiable.

XVII

But from the interview what flowed?
Alas! It is not hard to guess.
The insensate fire of love still glowed
Nor discontinued to distress
A spirit which for sorrow yearned.
Tattiana more than ever burned
With hopeless passion: from her bed
Sweet slumber winged its way and fled.
Her health, life's sweetness and its
  bloom,
Her smile and maidenly repose,
All vanished as an echo goes.
Across her youth a shade had come,
As when the tempest's veil is drawn
Across the smiling face of dawn.

XVIII

Alas! Tattiana fades away,
Grows pale and sinks, but nothing says;
Listless is she the livelong day

Nor interest in aught betrays.
Shaking with serious air the head,
In whispers low the neighbours said:
'Tis time she to the altar went!
But enough! Now, 'tis my intent
The imagination to enliven
With love which happiness extends;
Against my inclination, friends,
By sympathy I have been driven.
Forgive me! Such the love I bear
My heroine, Tattiana dear.

XIX

Vladimir, hourly more a slave
To youthful Olga's beauty bright,
Into delicious bondage gave
His ardent soul with full delight.
Always together, eventide
Found them in darkness side by side,
At morn, hand clasped in hand, they rove
Around the meadow and the grove.
And what resulted? Drunk with love,

But with confused and bashful air,
Lenski at intervals would dare,
If Olga smilingly approve,
Dally with a dishevelled tress
Or kiss the border of her dress.

XX

To Olga frequently he would
Some nice instructive novel read,
Whose author nature understood
Better than Chateaubriand did
Yet sometimes pages two or three
(Nonsense and pure absurdity,
For maiden's hearing deemed unfit),
He somewhat blushing would omit:
Far from the rest the pair would creep
And (elbows on the table) they
A game of chess would often play,
Buried in meditation deep,
Till absently Vladimir took
With his own pawn alas! his rook!

XXI

Homeward returning, he at home
Is occupied with Olga fair,
An album, fly-leaf of the tome,
He leisurely adorns for her.
Landscapes thereon he would design,
A tombstone, Aphrodite's shrine,
Or, with a pen and colours fit,
A dove which on a lyre doth sit;
The "in memoriam" pages sought,
Where many another hand had signed
A tender couplet he combined,
A register of fleeting thought,
A flimsy trace of musings past
Which might for many ages last.

XXII

Surely ye all have overhauled
A country damsel's album trim,
Which all her darling friends have
  scrawled

From first to last page to the rim.
Behold! orthography despising,
Metreless verses recognizing
By friendship how they were abused,
Hewn, hacked, and otherwise ill-used.
Upon the opening page ye find:
Qu'ecrirer-vouz sur ces tablettes?
Subscribed, **toujours à vous, Annette;**
And on the last one, underlined:
Who in thy love finds more delight
Beyond this may attempt to write.

XXIII

Infallibly you there will find
Two hearts, a torch, of flowers a wreath,
And vows will probably be signed:
Affectionately yours till death.
Some army poet therein may
Have smuggled his flagitious lay.
In such an album with delight
I would, my friends, inscriptions write,
Because I should be sure, meanwhile,

My verses, kindly meant, would earn
Delighted glances in return;
That afterwards with evil smile
They would not solemnly debate
If cleverly or not I prate.

XXIV

But, O ye tomes without compare,
Which from the devil's bookcase start,
Albums magnificent which scare
The fashionable rhymester's heart!
Yea! although rendered beauteous
By Tolstoy's pencil marvellous,
Though Baratynski verses penned,[45]
The thunderbolt on you descend!
Whene'er a brilliant courtly dame
Presents her quarto amiably,
Despair and anger seize on me,

[45] Count Tolstoy, a celebrated artist who subsequently became Vice-President of the Academy of Arts at St. Petersburg. Baratynski, see Note 43.

And a malicious epigram
Trembles upon my lips from spite, –
And madrigals I'm asked to write!

XXV

But Lenski madrigals ne'er wrote
In Olga's album, youthful maid,
To purest love he tuned his note
Nor frigid adulation paid.
What never was remarked or heard
Of Olga he in song averred;
His elegies, which plenteous streamed,
Both natural and truthful seemed.
Thus thou, Yazykoff, dost arise[46]
In amorous flights when so inspired,
Singing God knows what maid admired,
And all thy precious elegies,
Sometime collected, shall relate
The story of thy life and fate.

---

[46] Yazykoff, a poet contemporary with Pushkin. He was an author of promise – unfulfilled.

XXVI

Since Fame and Freedom he adored,
Incited by his stormy Muse
Odes Lenski also had outpoured,
But Olga would not such peruse.
When poets lachrymose recite
Beneath the eyes of ladies bright
Their own productions, some insist
No greater pleasure can exist
Just so! that modest swain is blest
Who reads his visionary theme
To the fair object of his dream,
A beauty languidly at rest,
Yes, happy – though she at his side
By other thoughts be occupied.

XXVII

But I the products of my Muse,
Consisting of harmonious lays,
To my old nurse alone peruse,
Companion of my childhood's days.

Or, after dinner's dull repast,
I by the button-hole seize fast
My neighbour, who by chance drew near,
And breathe a drama in his ear.
Or else (I deal not here in jokes),
Exhausted by my woes and rhymes,
I sail upon my lake at times
And terrify a swarm of ducks,
Who, heard the music of my lay,
Take to their wings and fly away.

XXVIII

But to Onéguine! **A propos!**
Friends, I must your indulgence pray.
His daily occupations, lo!
Minutely I will now portray.
A hermit's life Onéguine led,
At seven in summer rose from bed,
And clad in airy costume took
His course unto the running brook.
There, aping Gulnare's bard, he spanned
His Hellespont from bank to bank,

And then a cup of coffee drank,
Some wretched journal in his hand;
Then dressed himself...

[Note: Stanza left unfinished by the author.]

XXIX

Sound sleep, books, walking, were his bliss,
The murmuring brook, the woodland shade,
The uncontaminated kiss
Of a young dark-eyed country maid,
A fiery, yet well-broken horse,
A dinner, whimsical each course,
A bottle of a vintage white
And solitude and calm delight.
Such was Onéguine's sainted life,
And such unconsciously he led,
Nor marked how summer's prime had fled

In aimless ease and far from strife,
The curse of commonplace delight.
And town and friends forgotten quite.

XXX

This northern summer of our own,
On winters of the south a skit,
Glimmers and dies. This is well known,
Though we will not acknowledge it.
Already Autumn chilled the sky,
The tiny sun shone less on high
And shorter had the days become.
The forests in mysterious gloom
Were stripped with melancholy sound,
Upon the earth a mist did lie
And many a caravan on high
Of clamorous geese flew southward bound.
A weary season was at hand –
November at the gate did stand.

XXXI

The morn arises foggy, cold,
The silent fields no peasant nears,
The wolf upon the highways bold
With his ferocious mate appears.
Detecting him the passing horse
Snorts, and his rider bends his course
And wisely gallops to the hill.
No more at dawn the shepherd will
Drive out the cattle from their shed,
Nor at the hour of noon with sound
Of horn in circle call them round.
Singing inside her hut the maid
Spins, whilst the friend of wintry night,
The pine-torch, by her crackles bright.

XXXII

Already crisp hoar frosts impose
O'er all a sheet of silvery dust
(Readers expect the rhyme of **rose**,
There! take it quickly, if ye must).

Behold! than polished floor more nice
The shining river clothed in ice;
A joyous troop of little boys
Engrave the ice with strident noise.
A heavy goose on scarlet feet,
Thinking to float upon the stream,
Descends the bank with care extreme,
But staggers, slips, and falls. We greet
The first bright wreathing storm of snow
Which falls in starry flakes below.

XXXIII

How in the country pass this time?
Walking? The landscape tires the eye
In winter by its blank and dim
And naked uniformity.
On horseback gallop o'er the steppe!
Your steed, though rough-shod, cannot
  keep
His footing on the treacherous rime
And may fall headlong any time.
Alone beneath your rooftree stay

And read De Pradt or Walter Scott![47]
Keep your accounts! You'd rather not?
Then get mad drunk or wroth; the day
Will pass; the same to-morrow try –
You'll spend your winter famously!

XXXIV

A true Childe Harold my Eugene
To idle musing was a prey;
At morn an icy bath within
He sat, and then the livelong day,
Alone within his habitation
And buried deep in meditation,
He round the billiard-table stalked,
The balls impelled, the blunt cue chalked;
When evening o'er the landscape looms,
Billiards abandoned, cue forgot,

---

[47] The Abbé de Pradt: b. 1759, d. 1837. A political pamphleteer of the French Revolution: was at first an emigre, but made his peace with Napoleon and was appointed Archbishop of Malines.

A table to the fire is brought,
And he waits dinner. Lenski comes,
Driving abreast three horses gray.
"Bring dinner now without delay!"

XXXV

Upon the table in a trice
Of widow Clicquot or Moet
A blessed bottle, placed in ice,
For the young poet they display.
Like Hippocrene it scatters light,
Its ebullition foaming white
(Like other things I could relate)
My heart of old would captivate.
The last poor obol I was worth –
Was it not so? – for thee I gave,
And thy inebriating wave
Full many a foolish prank brought forth;
And oh! what verses, what delights,
Delicious visions, jests and fights!

XXXVI

Alas! my stomach it betrays
With its exhilarating flow,
And I confess that now-a-days
I prefer sensible Bordeaux.
To cope with Ay no more I dare,
For Ay is like a mistress fair,
Seductive, animated, bright,
But wilful, frivolous, and light.
But thou, Bordeaux, art like the friend
Who in the agony of grief
Is ever ready with relief,
Assistance ever will extend,
Or quietly partake our woe.
All hail! my good old friend Bordeaux!

XXXVII

The fire sinks low. An ashy cloak
The golden ember now enshrines,
And barely visible the smoke
Upward in a thin stream inclines.

But little warmth the fireplace lends,
Tobacco smoke the flue ascends,
The goblet still is bubbling bright –
Outside descend the mists of night.
How pleasantly the evening jogs
When o'er a glass with friends we prate
Just at the hour we designate
The time between the wolf and dogs –
I cannot tell on what pretence –
But lo! the friends to chat commence.

XXXVIII

"How are our neighbours fair, pray tell,
Tattiana, saucy Olga thine?" –
"The family are all quite well –
Give me just half a glass of wine –
They sent their compliments – but oh!
How charming Olga's shoulders grow!
Her figure perfect grows with time!
She is an angel! We sometime
Must visit them. Come! you must own,
My friend, 'tis but to pay a debt,

For twice you came to them and yet
You never since your nose have shown.
But stay! A dolt am I who speak!
They have invited you this week."

XXXIX

"Me?" – "Yes! It is Tattiana's fête
Next Saturday. The Làrina
Told me to ask you. Ere that date
Make up your mind to go there." – "Ah!
It will be by a mob beset
Of every sort and every set!" –
"Not in the least, assured am I!" –
"Who will be there?" – "The family.
Do me a favour and appear.
Will you?" – "Agreed." – "I thank you,
 friend,"
And saying this Vladimir drained
His cup unto his maiden dear.
Then touching Olga they depart
In fresh discourse. Such, love, thou art!

XL

He was most gay. The happy date
In three weeks would arrive for them;
The secrets of the marriage state
And love's delicious diadem
With rapturous longing he awaits,
Nor in his dreams anticipates
Hymen's embarrassments, distress,
And freezing fits of weariness.
Though we, of Hymen foes, meanwhile,
In life domestic see a string
Of pictures painful harrowing,
A novel in Lafontaine's style,
My wretched Lenski's fate I mourn,
He seemed for matrimony born.

XLI

He was beloved: or say at least,
He thought so, and existence charmed.
The credulous indeed are blest,
And he who, jealousy disarmed,

In sensual sweets his soul doth steep
As drunken tramps at nightfall sleep,
Or, parable more flattering,
As butterflies to blossoms cling.
But wretched who anticipates,
Whose brain no fond illusions daze,
Who every gesture, every phrase
In true interpretation hates:
Whose heart experience icy made
And yet oblivion forbade.

END OF CANTO THE FOURTH

Canto the Fifth

The Fête

‘Oh, do not dream these fearful dreams,
  O my Svetlana.’ – Joukóvski

Canto The Fifth

[Note: Mikhailovskoe, 1825-6]

I

That year the autumn season late
Kept lingering on as loath to go,
All Nature winter seemed to await,
Till January fell no snow –
The third at night. Tattiana wakes
Betimes, and sees, when morning breaks,
Park, garden, palings, yard below
And roofs near morn blanched o'er with snow;
Upon the windows tracery,
The trees in silvery array,
Down in the courtyard magpies gay,
And the far mountains daintily
O'erspread with Winter's carpet bright,
All so distinct, and all so white!

II

Winter! The peasant blithely goes
To labour in his sledge forgot,

His pony sniffing the fresh snows
Just manages a feeble trot
Though deep he sinks into the drift;
Forth the **kibitka** gallops swift,[48]
Its driver seated on the rim
In scarlet sash and sheepskin trim;
Yonder the household lad doth run,
Placed in a sledge his terrier black,
Himself transformed into a hack;
To freeze his finger hath begun,
He laughs, although it aches from cold,
His mother from the door doth scold.

III

In scenes like these it may be though,
Ye feel but little interest,
They are all natural and low,
Are not with elegance impressed.
Another bard with art divine

[48] The "kibitka," properly speaking, whether on wheels or runners, is a vehicle with a hood not unlike a big cradle.

Hath pictured in his gorgeous line
The first appearance of the snows
And all the joys which Winter knows.
He will delight you, I am sure,
When he in ardent verse portrays
Secret excursions made in sleighs;
But competition I abjure
Either with him or thee in song,
Bard of the Finnish maiden young.[49]

IV

Tattiana, Russian to the core,
Herself not knowing well the reason,
The Russian winter did adore
And the cold beauties of the season:
On sunny days the glistening rime,
Sledging, the snows, which at the time

---

[49] The allusions in the foregoing stanza are in the first place to a poem entitled "The First Snow," by Prince Viazemski and secondly to "Eda," by Baratynski, a poem descriptive of life in Finland.

Of sunset glow with rosy light,
The misty evenings ere Twelfth Night.
These evenings as in days of old
The Làrinas would celebrate,
The servants used to congregate
And the young ladies fortunes told,
And every year distributed
Journeys and warriors to wed.

V

Tattiana in traditions old
Believed, the people's wisdom weird,
In dreams and what the moon foretold
And what she from the cards inferred.
Omens inspired her soul with fear,
Mysteriously all objects near
A hidden meaning could impart,
Presentiments oppressed her heart.
Lo! the prim cat upon the stove
With one paw strokes her face and
  purrs,
Tattiana certainly infers

That guests approach: and when above
The new moon's crescent slim she spied,
Suddenly to the left hand side,

VI

She trembled and grew deadly pale.
Or a swift meteor, may be,
Across the gloom of heaven would sail
And disappear in space; then she
Would haste in agitation dire
To mutter her concealed desire
Ere the bright messenger had set.
When in her walks abroad she met
A friar black approaching near,[50]
Or a swift hare from mead to mead

---

[50] The Russian clergy are divided into two classes: the white or secular, which is made up of the mass of parish priests, and the black who inhabit the monasteries, furnish the high dignitaries of the Church, and constitute that swarm of useless drones for whom Peter the Great felt such a deep repugnance.

Had run across her path at speed,
Wholly beside herself with fear,
Anticipating woe she pined,
Certain misfortune near opined.

VII

Wherefore? She found a secret joy
In horror for itself alone,
Thus Nature doth our souls alloy,
Thus her perversity hath shown.
Twelfth Night approaches. Merry eves![51]
When thoughtless youth whom nothing
  grieves,
Before whose inexperienced sight
Life lies extended, vast and bright,
To peer into the future tries.
Old age through spectacles too peers,

---

51 Refers to the "Sviatki" or Holy Nights between Christmas Eve and Twelfth Night. Divination, or the telling of fortunes by various expedients, is the favourite pastime on these occasions.

Although the destined coffin nears,
Having lost all in life we prize.
It matters not. Hope e'en to these
With childlike lisp will lie to please.

VIII

Tattiana gazed with curious eye
On melted wax in water poured;
The clue unto some mystery
She deemed its outline might afford.
Rings from a dish of water full
In order due the maidens pull;
But when Tattiana's hand had ta'en
A ring she heard the ancient strain:
The peasants there are rich as kings,
They shovel silver with a spade,
He whom we sing to shall be made
Happy and glorious. But this brings
With sad refrain misfortune near.
Girls the **kashourka** much prefer.[52]

---

[52] During the "sviatki" it is a common custom for the girls to assemble around a table on which

IX

Frosty the night; the heavens shone;
The wondrous host of heavenly spheres
Sailed silently in unison –
Tattiana in the yard appears
In a half-open dressing-gown
And bends her mirror on the moon,
But trembling on the mirror dark
The sad moon only could remark.
List! the snow crunches – he draws nigh!
The girl on tiptoe forward bounds
And her voice sweeter than the sounds

---

is placed a dish or basin of water which contains a ring. Each in her turn extracts the ring from the basin whilst the remainder sing in chorus the "podbliudni pessni," or "dish songs" before mentioned. These are popularly supposed to indicate the fortunes of the immediate holder of the ring. The first-named lines foreshadow death; the latter, the "kashourka," or "kitten song," indicates approaching marriage. It commences thus: "The cat asked the kitten to sleep on the stove."

Of clarinet or flute doth cry:
"What is your name?" The boor looked dazed,
And "Agathon" replied, amazed.[53]

X

Tattiana (nurse the project planned)
By night prepared for sorcery,
And in the bathroom did command
To lay two covers secretly.
But sudden fear assailed Tattiana,
And I, remembering Svetlana,[54]
Become alarmed. So never mind!
I'm not for witchcraft now inclined.
So she her silken sash unlaced,
Undressed herself and went to bed
And soon Lel hovered o'er her head.[55]

---

[53] The superstition is that the name of the future husband may thus be discovered.

[54] See Note 30.

[55] Lel, in Slavonic mythology, corresponds to the Morpheus of the Latins. The word is

Beneath her downy pillow placed,
A little virgin mirror peeps.
'Tis silent all. Tattiana sleeps.

XI

A dreadful sleep Tattiana sleeps.
She dreamt she journeyed o'er a field
All covered up with snow in heaps,
By melancholy fogs concealed.
Amid the snowdrifts which surround
A stream, by winter's ice unbound,
Impetuously clove its way
With boiling torrent dark and gray;
Two poles together glued by ice,
A fragile bridge and insecure,
Spanned the unbridled torrent o'er;
Beside the thundering abyss
Tattiana in despair unfeigned
Rooted unto the spot remained.

---

evidently connected with the verb "leleyat" to fondle or soothe, likewise with our own word "to lull."

XII

As if against obstruction sore
Tattiana o'er the stream complained;
To help her to the other shore
No one appeared to lend a hand.
But suddenly a snowdrift stirs,
And what from its recess appears?
A bristly bear of monstrous size!
He roars, and "Ah!" Tattiana cries.
He offers her his murderous paw;
She nerves herself from her alarm
And leans upon the monster's arm,
With footsteps tremulous with awe
Passes the torrent But alack!
Bruin is marching at her back!

XIII

She, to turn back her eyes afraid,
Accelerates her hasty pace,
But cannot anyhow evade
Her shaggy myrmidon in chase.

The bear rolls on with many a grunt:
A forest now she sees in front
With fir-trees standing motionless
In melancholy loveliness,
Their branches by the snow bowed down.
Through aspens, limes and birches bare,
The shining orbs of night appear;
There is no path; the storm hath strewn
Both bush and brake, ravine and steep,
And all in snow is buried deep.

XIV

The wood she enters – bear behind, –
In snow she sinks up to the knee;
Now a long branch itself entwined
Around her neck, now violently
Away her golden earrings tore;
Now the sweet little shoes she wore,
Grown clammy, stick fast in the snow;
Her handkerchief she loses now;
No time to pick it up! afraid,
She hears the bear behind her press,

Nor dares the skirting of her dress
For shame lift up the modest maid.
She runs, the bear upon her trail,
Until her powers of running fail.

XV

She sank upon the snow. But Bruin
Adroitly seized and carried her;
Submissive as if in a swoon,
She cannot draw a breath or stir.
He dragged her by a forest road
Till amid trees a hovel showed,
By barren snow heaped up and bound,
A tangled wilderness around.
Bright blazed the window of the place,
Within resounded shriek and shout:
"My chum lives here," Bruin grunts out.
"Warm yourself here a little space!"
Straight for the entrance then he made
And her upon the threshold laid.

XVI

Recovering, Tania gazes round;
Bear gone – she at the threshold placed;
Inside clink glasses, cries resound
As if it were some funeral feast.
But deeming all this nonsense pure,
She peeped through a chink of the door.
What doth she see? Around the board
Sit many monstrous shapes abhorred.
A canine face with horns thereon,
Another with cock's head appeared,
Here an old witch with hirsute beard,
There an imperious skeleton;
A dwarf adorned with tail, again
A shape half cat and half a crane.

XVII

Yet ghastlier, yet more wonderful,
A crab upon a spider rides,
Perched on a goose's neck a skull
In scarlet cap revolving glides.

A windmill too a jig performs
And wildly waves its arms and storms;
Barking, songs, whistling, laughter
  coarse,
The speech of man and tramp of horse.
But wide Tattiana oped her eyes
When in that company she saw
Him who inspired both love and awe,
The hero we immortalize.
Onéguine sat the table by
And viewed the door with cunning eye.

XVIII

All bustle when he makes a sign:
He drinks, all drink and loudly call;
He smiles, in laughter all combine;
He knits his brows – 'tis silent all.
He there is master – that is plain;
Tattiana courage doth regain
And grown more curious by far
Just placed the entrance door ajar.
The wind rose instantly, blew out

The fire of the nocturnal lights;
A trouble fell upon the sprites;
Onéguine lightning glances shot;
Furious he from the table rose;
All arise. To the door he goes.

XIX

Terror assails her. Hastily
Tattiana would attempt to fly,
She cannot – then impatiently
She strains her throat to force a cry –
She cannot – Eugene oped the door
And the young girl appeared before
Those hellish phantoms. Peals arise
Of frantic laughter, and all eyes
And hoofs and crooked snouts and
  paws,
Tails which a bushy tuft adorns,
Whiskers and bloody tongues and horns,
Sharp rows of tushes, bony claws,
Are turned upon her. All combine

In one great shout: she's mine! she's
mine!

XX

"Mine!" cried Eugene with savage tone.
The troop of apparitions fled,
And in the frosty night alone
Remained with him the youthful maid.
With tranquil air Onéguine leads
Tattiana to a corner, bids
Her on a shaky bench sit down;
His head sinks slowly, rests upon
Her shoulder – Olga swiftly came –
And Lenski followed – a light broke –
His fist Onéguine fiercely shook
And gazed around with eyes of flame;
The unbidden guests he roughly
chides –
Tattiana motionless abides.

XXI

The strife grew furious and Eugene
Grasped a long knife and instantly
Struck Lenski dead – across the scene
Dark shadows thicken – a dread cry
Was uttered, and the cabin shook –
Tattiana terrified awoke.
She gazed around her – it was day.
Lo! through the frozen windows play
Aurora's ruddy rays of light –
The door flew open – Olga came,
More blooming than the Boreal flame
And swifter than the swallow's flight.
"Come," she cried, "sister, tell me e'en
Whom you in slumber may have seen."

XXII

But she, her sister never heeding,
With book in hand reclined in bed,
Page after page continued reading,
But no reply unto her made.

Although her book did not contain
The bard's enthusiastic strain,
Nor precepts sage nor pictures e'en,
Yet neither Virgil nor Racine
Nor Byron, Walter Scott, nor Seneca,
Nor the **Journal des Modes**, I vouch,
Ever absorbed a maid so much:
Its name, my friends, was Martin Zadeka,
The chief of the Chaldean wise,
Who dreams expound and prophecies.

XXIII

Brought by a pedlar vagabond
Unto their solitude one day,
This monument of thought profound
Tattiana purchased with a stray
Tome of "Malvina," and but three[56]
And a half rubles down gave she;
Also, to equalise the scales,
She got a book of nursery tales,

56 "Malvina," a romance by Madame Cottin.

A grammar, likewise Petriads two,
Marmontel also, tome the third;
Tattiana every day conferred
With Martin Zadeka. In woe
She consolation thence obtained –
Inseparable they remained.

XXIV

The dream left terror in its train.
Not knowing its interpretation,
Tania the meaning would obtain
Of such a dread hallucination.
Tattiana to the index flies
And alphabetically tries
The words **bear, bridge, fir, darkness, bog,**
Raven, snowstorm, tempest, fog,
Et cetera; but nothing showed
Her Martin Zadeka in aid,
Though the foul vision promise made
Of a most mournful episode,

And many a day thereafter laid
A load of care upon the maid.

XXV

"But lo! forth from the valleys dun
With purple hand Aurora leads,
Swift following in her wake, the sun,"[57]
And a grand festival proceeds.
The Làrinas were since sunrise
O'erwhelmed with guests; by families
The neighbours come, in sledge
  approach,
Britzka, kibitka, or in coach.
Crush and confusion in the hall,
Latest arrivals' salutations,
Barking, young ladies' osculations,
Shouts, laughter, jamming 'gainst the
  wall,

---

[57] The above three lines are a parody on the turgid style of Lomonossoff, a literary man of the second Catherine's era.

Bows and the scrape of many feet,
Nurses who scream and babes who
bleat.

XXVI

Bringing his partner corpulent
Fat Poustiakoff drove to the door;
Gvozdine, a landlord excellent,
Oppressor of the wretched poor;
And the Skatènines, aged pair,
With all their progeny were there,
Who from two years to thirty tell;
Pétòushkoff, the provincial swell;
Bouyànoff too, my cousin, wore[58]
His wadded coat and cap with peak
(Surely you know him as I speak);
And Fliànoff, pensioned councillor,
Rogue and extortioner of yore,
Now buffoon, glutton, and a bore.

---

[58] Pushkin calls Bouyànoff his cousin because he is a character in the "Dangerous Neighbour," a poem by Vassili Pushkin, the poet's uncle.

XXVII

The family of Kharlikoff,
Came with Monsieur Triquet, a prig,
Who arrived lately from Tamboff,
In spectacles and chestnut wig.
Like a true Frenchman, couplets wrought
In Tania's praise in pouch he brought,
Known unto children perfectly:
Reveillez-vouz, belle endormie.
Among some ancient ballads thrust,
He found them in an almanac,
And the sagacious Triquet back
To light had brought them from their dust,
Whilst he "belle Nina" had the face
By "belle Tattiana" to replace.

XXVIII

Lo! from the nearest barrack came,
Of old maids the divinity,
And comfort of each country dame,
The captain of a company.

He enters. Ah! good news to-day!
The military band will play.
The colonel sent it. Oh! delight!
So there will be a dance to-night.
Girls in anticipation skip!
But dinner-time comes. Two and two
They hand in hand to table go.
The maids beside Tattiana keep –
Men opposite. The cross they sign
And chattering loud sit down to dine.

XXIX

Ceased for a space all chattering.
Jaws are at work. On every side
Plates, knives and forks are clattering
And ringing wine-glasses are plied.
But by degrees the crowd begin
To raise a clamour and a din:
They laugh, they argue, and they bawl,
They shout and no one lists at all.
The doors swing open: Lenski makes
His entrance with Onéguine. "Ah!

At last the author!" cries Mamma.
The guests make room; aside each takes
His chair, plate, knife and fork in haste;
The friends are called and quickly placed.

XXX

Right opposite Tattiana placed,
She, than the morning moon more pale,
More timid than a doe long chased,
Lifts not her eyes which swimming fail.
Anew the flames of passion start
Within her; she is sick at heart;
The two friends' compliments she hears
Not, and a flood of bitter tears
With effort she restrains. Well nigh
The poor girl fell into a faint,
But strength of mind and self-restraint
Prevailed at last. She in reply
Said something in an undertone
And at the table sat her down.

XXXI

To tragedy, the fainting fit,
And female tears hysterical,
Onéguine could not now submit,
For long he had endured them all.
Our misanthrope was full of ire,
At a great feast against desire,
And marking Tania's agitation,
Cast down his eyes in trepidation
And sulked in silent indignation;
Swearing how Lenski he would rile,
Avenge himself in proper style.
Triumphant by anticipation,
Caricatures he now designed
Of all the guests within his mind.

XXXII

Certainly not Eugene alone
Tattiana's trouble might have spied,
But that the eyes of every one
By a rich pie were occupied –

Unhappily too salt by far;
And that a bottle sealed with tar
Appeared, Don's effervescing boast,[59]
Between the blanc-mange and the roast;
Behind, of glasses an array,
Tall, slender, like thy form designed,
Zizi, thou mirror of my mind,
Fair object of my guileless lay,
Seductive cup of love, whose flow
Made me so tipsy long ago!

XXXIII

From the moist cork the bottle freed
With loud explosion, the bright wine
Hissed forth. With serious air indeed,
Long tortured by his lay divine,
Triquet arose, and for the bard
The company deep silence guard.
Tania well nigh expired when he

---

59 The Donskoe Champanskoe is a species of sparkling wine manufactured in the vicinity of the river Don.

Turned to her and discordantly
Intoned it, manuscript in hand.
Voices and hands applaud, and she
Must bow in common courtesy;
The poet, modest though so grand,
Drank to her health in the first place,
Then handed her the song with grace.

XXXIV

Congratulations, toasts resound,
Tattiana thanks to all returned,
But, when Onéguine's turn came round,
The maiden's weary eye which yearned,
Her agitation and distress
Aroused in him some tenderness.
He bowed to her nor silence broke,
But somehow there shone in his look
The witching light of sympathy;
I know not if his heart felt pain
Or if he meant to flirt again,
From habit or maliciously,

But kindness from his eye had beamed
And to revive Tattiana seemed.

XXXV

The chairs are thrust back with a roar,
The crowd unto the drawing-room
  speeds,
As bees who leave their dainty store
And seek in buzzing swarms the meads.
Contented and with victuals stored,
Neighbour by neighbour sat and snored,
Matrons unto the fireplace go,
Maids in the corner whisper low;
Behold! green tables are brought forth,
And testy gamesters do engage
In boston and the game of age,
Ombre, and whist all others worth:
A strong resemblance these possess –
All sons of mental weariness.

XXXVI

Eight rubbers were already played,
Eight times the heroes of the fight
Change of position had essayed,
When tea was brought. 'Tis my delight
Time to denote by dinner, tea,
And supper. In the country we
Can count the time without much fuss –
The stomach doth admonish us.
And, by the way, I here assert
That for that matter in my verse
As many dinners I rehearse,
As oft to meat and drink advert,
As thou, great Homer, didst of yore,
Whom thirty centuries adore.

XXXVII

I will with thy divinity
Contend with knife and fork and platter,
But grant with magnanimity
I'm beaten in another matter;

Thy heroes, sanguinary wights,
Also thy rough-and-tumble fights,
Thy Venus and thy Jupiter,
More advantageously appear
Than cold Onéguine's oddities,
The aspect of a landscape drear.
Or e'en Istomina, my dear,
And fashion's gay frivolities;
But my Tattiana, on my soul,
Is sweeter than thy Helen foul.

XXXVIII

No one the contrary will urge,
Though for his Helen Menelaus
Again a century should scourge
Us, and like Trojan warriors slay us;
Though around honoured Priam's throne
Troy's sages should in concert own
Once more, when she appeared in sight,
Paris and Menelaus right.
But as to fighting – 'twill appear!
For patience, reader, I must plead!

A little farther please to read
And be not in advance severe.
There'll be a fight. I do not lie.
My word of honour given have I.

XXXIX

The tea, as I remarked, appeared,
But scarce had maids their saucers ta'en
When in the grand saloon was heard
Of bassoons and of flutes the strain.
His soul by crash of music fired,
His tea with rum no more desired,
The Paris of those country parts
To Olga Petoushkova darts:
To Tania Lenski; Kharlikova,
A marriageable maid matured,
The poet from Tamboff secured,
Bouyànoff whisked off Poustiakova.
All to the grand saloon are gone –
The ball in all its splendour shone.

XL

I tried when I began this tale,
(See the first canto if ye will),
A ball in Peter's capital,
To sketch ye in Albano's style.[60]
But by fantastic dreams distraught,
My memory wandered wide and sought
The feet of my dear lady friends.
O feet, where'er your path extends
I long enough deceived have erred.
The perfidies I recollect
Should make me much more circumspect,
Reform me both in deed and word,
And this fifth canto ought to be
From such digressions wholly free.

XLI

The whirlwind of the waltz sweeps by,

60 Francesco Albano, a celebrated painter, styled the "Anacreon of Painting," was born at Bologna 1578, and died in the year 1666.

Undeviating and insane
As giddy youth's hilarity –
Pair after pair the race sustain.
The moment for revenge, meanwhile,
Espying, Eugene with a smile
Approaches Olga and the pair
Amid the company career.
Soon the maid on a chair he seats,
Begins to talk of this and that,
But when two minutes she had sat,
Again the giddy waltz repeats.
All are amazed; but Lenski he
Scarce credits what his eyes can see.

XLII

Hark! the mazurka. In times past,
When the mazurka used to peal,
All rattled in the ball-room vast,
The parquet cracked beneath the heel,
And jolting jarred the window-frames.
'Tis not so now. Like gentle dames
We glide along a floor of wax.

However, the mazurka lacks
Nought of its charms original
In country towns, where still it keeps
Its stamping, capers and high leaps.
Fashion is there immutable,
Who tyrannizes us with ease,
Of modern Russians the disease.

XLIII

Bouyànoff, wrathful cousin mine,
Unto the hero of this lay
Olga and Tania led. Malign,
Onéguine Olga bore away.
Gliding in negligent career,
He bending whispered in her ear
Some madrigal not worth a rush,
And pressed her hand – the crimson blush
Upon her cheek by adulation
Grew brighter still. But Lenski hath
Seen all, beside himself with wrath,
And hot with jealous indignation,

Till the mazurka's close he stays,
Her hand for the cotillon prays.

XLIV

She fears she cannot. – Cannot?
  Why? –
She promised Eugene, or she would
With great delight. – O God on high!
Heard he the truth? And thus she
  could –
And can it be? But late a child
And now a fickle flirt and wild,
Cunning already to display
And well-instructed to betray!
Lenski the stroke could not sustain,
At womankind he growled a curse,
Departed, ordered out his horse
And galloped home. But pistols twain,
A pair of bullets – nought beside –
His fate shall presently decide.

Canto the Sixth

The Duel

‘La, sotto giorni nubilosi e brevi,
Nasce una gente a cui ’l morir non duole.’
Petrarch

Canto The Sixth

[Mikhailovskoe, 1826: the two final
stanzas were, however,
written at Moscow.]

I

Having remarked Vladimir's flight,
Onéguine, bored to death again,
By Olga stood, dejected quite
And satisfied with vengeance ta'en.
Olga began to long likewise
For Lenski, sought him with her eyes,
And endless the cotillon seemed
As if some troubled dream she
  dreamed.
'Tis done. To supper they proceed.
Bedding is laid out and to all
Assigned a lodging, from the hall[61]

---

[61] Hospitality is a national virtue of the Russians. On festal occasions in the country the whole party is usually accommodated for the night, or indeed for as many nights as desired, within the house of the entertainer. This of course is rendered necessary by the great distances which separate the residences of the gentry. Still, the alacrity with which a Russian hostess will turn her house topsy-turvy for the accommodation

Up to the attic, and all need
Tranquil repose. Eugene alone
To pass the night at home hath gone.

II

All slumber. In the drawing-room
Loud snores the cumbrous Poustiakoff
With better half as cumbersome;
Gvozdine, Bouyànoff, Pétòushkoff
And Fliànoff, somewhat indisposed,
On chairs in the saloon reposed,
Whilst on the floor Monsieur Triquet
In jersey and in nightcap lay.
In Olga's and Tattiana's rooms
Lay all the girls by sleep embraced,
Except one by the window placed
Whom pale Diana's ray illumes –
My poor Tattiana cannot sleep
But stares into the darkness deep.

---

of forty or fifty guests would somewhat astonish the mistress of a modern Belgravian mansion.

III

His visit she had not awaited,
His momentary loving glance
Her inmost soul had penetrated,
And his strange conduct at the dance
With Olga; nor of this appeared
An explanation: she was scared,
Alarmed by jealous agonies:
A hand of ice appeared to seize[62]
Her heart: it seemed a darksome pit
Beneath her roaring opened wide:
"I shall expire," Tattiana cried,
"But death from him will be delight.

---

62 There must be a peculiar appropriateness in this expression as descriptive of the sensation of extreme cold. Mr. Wallace makes use of an identical phrase in describing an occasion when he was frostbitten whilst sledging in Russia. He says (vol. i. p. 33): "My fur cloak flew open, the cold seemed to grasp me in the region of the heart, and I fell insensible."

I murmur not! Why mournfulness?
He **cannot** give me happiness."

IV

Haste, haste thy lagging pace, my story!
A new acquaintance we must scan.
There dwells five versts from Krasnogory,
Vladimir's property, a man
Who thrives this moment as I write,
A philosophic anchorite:
Zaretski, once a bully bold,
A gambling troop when he controlled,
Chief rascal, pot-house president,
Now of a family the head,
Simple and kindly and unwed,
True friend, landlord benevolent,
Yea! and a man of honour, lo!
How perfect doth our epoch grow!

V

Time was the flattering voice of fame,

His ruffian bravery adored,
And true, his pistol's faultless aim
An ace at fifteen paces bored.
But I must add to what I write
That, tipsy once in actual fight,
He from his Kalmuck horse did leap
In mud and mire to wallow deep,
Drunk as a fly; and thus the French
A valuable hostage gained,
A modern Regulus unchained,
Who to surrender did not blench
That every morn at Verrey's cost
Three flasks of wine he might exhaust.

VI

Time was, his raillery was gay,
He loved the simpleton to mock,
To make wise men the idiot play
Openly or 'neath decent cloak.
Yet sometimes this or that deceit
Encountered punishment complete,
And sometimes into snares as well

Himself just like a greenhorn fell.
He could in disputation shine
With pungent or obtuse retort,
At times to silence would resort,
At times talk nonsense with design;
Quarrels among young friends he bred
And to the field of honour led;

VII

Or reconciled them, it may be,
And all the three to breakfast went;
Then he'd malign them secretly
With jest and gossip gaily blent.
Sed alia tempora. And bravery
(Like love, another sort of knavery!)
Diminishes as years decline.
But, as I said, Zaretski mine
Beneath acacias, cherry-trees,
From storms protection having sought,
Lived as a really wise man ought,
Like Horace, planted cabbages,

Both ducks and geese in plenty bred
And lessons to his children read.

VIII

He was no fool, and Eugene mine,
To friendship making no pretence,
Admired his judgment, which was fine,
Pervaded with much common sense.
He usually was glad to see
The man and liked his company,
So, when he came next day to call,
Was not surprised thereby at all.
But, after mutual compliments,
Zaretski with a knowing grin,
Ere conversation could begin,
The epistle from the bard presents.
Onéguine to the window went
And scanned in silence its content.

IX

It was a cheery, generous

Cartel, or challenge to a fight,
Whereto in language courteous
Lenski his comrade did invite.
Onéguine, by first impulse moved,
Turned and replied as it behoved,
Curtly announcing for the fray
That he was “ready any day.”
Zaretski rose, nor would explain,
He cared no longer there to stay,
Had much to do at home that day,
And so departed. But Eugene,
The matter by his conscience tried,
Was with himself dissatisfied.

X

In fact, the subject analysed,
Within that secret court discussed,
In much his conduct stigmatized;
For, from the outset, ’twas unjust
To jest as he had done last eve,
A timid, shrinking love to grieve.
And ought he not to disregard

The poet's madness? for 'tis hard
At eighteen not to play the fool!
Sincerely loving him, Eugene
Assuredly should not have been
Conventionality's dull tool –
Not a mere hot, pugnacious boy,
But man of sense and probity.

XI

He might his motives have narrated,
Not bristled up like a wild beast,
He ought to have conciliated
That youthful heart – "But, now at least,
The opportunity is flown.
Besides, a duellist well-known
Hath mixed himself in the affair,
Malicious and a slanderer.
Undoubtedly, disdain alone
Should recompense his idle jeers,
But fools – their calumnies and sneers" –

Behold! the world's opinion![63]
Our idol, Honour's motive force,
Round which revolves the universe.

XII

Impatient, boiling o'er with wrath,
The bard his answer waits at home,
But lo! his braggart neighbour hath
Triumphant with the answer come.
Now for the jealous youth what joy!
He feared the criminal might try
To treat the matter as a jest,
Use subterfuge, and thus his breast
From the dread pistol turn away.
But now all doubt was set aside,
Unto the windmill he must ride
To-morrow before break of day,
To cock the pistol; barrel bend
On thigh or temple, friend on friend.

---

63 A line of Griboyédoff's. (Woe from Wit.)

XIII

Resolved the flirt to cast away,
The foaming Lenski would refuse,
To see his Olga ere the fray –
His watch, the sun in turn he views –
Finally tost his arms in air
And lo! he is already there!
He deemed his coming would inspire
Olga with trepidation dire.
He was deceived. Just as before
The miserable bard to meet,
As hope uncertain and as sweet,
Olga ran skipping from the door.
She was as heedless and as gay –
Well! just as she was yesterday.

XIV

"Why did you leave last night so soon?"
Was the first question Olga made,
Lenski, into confusion thrown,
All silently hung down his head.

Jealousy and vexation took
To flight before her radiant look,
Before such fond simplicity
And mental elasticity.
He eyed her with a fond concern,
Perceived that he was still beloved,
Already by repentance moved
To ask forgiveness seemed to yearn;
But trembles, words he cannot find,
Delighted, almost sane in mind.

XV

But once more pensive and distressed
Beside his Olga doth he grieve,
Nor enough strength of mind possessed
To mention the foregoing eve,
He mused: "I will her saviour be!
With ardent sighs and flattery
The vile seducer shall not dare
The freshness of her heart impair,
Nor shall the caterpillar come
The lily's stem to eat away,

Nor shall the bud of yesterday
Perish when half disclosed its bloom!" –
All this, my friends, translate aright:
"I with my friend intend to fight!"

XVI

If he had only known the wound
Which rankled in Tattiana's breast,
And if Tattiana mine had found –
If the poor maiden could have guessed
That the two friends with morning's light
Above the yawning grave would fight, –
Ah! it may be, affection true
Had reconciled the pair anew!
But of this love, e'en casually,
As yet none had discovered aught;
Eugene of course related nought,
Tattiana suffered secretly;
Her nurse, who could have made a
  guess,
Was famous for thick-headedness.

XVII

Lenski that eve in thought immersed,
Now gloomy seemed and cheerful now,
But he who by the Muse was nursed
Is ever thus. With frowning brow
To the pianoforte he moves
And various chords upon it proves,
Then, eyeing Olga, whispers low:
"I'm happy, say, is it not so?" –
But it grew late; he must not stay;
Heavy his heart with anguish grew;
To the young girl he said adieu,
As it were, tore himself away.
Gazing into his face, she said:
"What ails thee?" – "Nothing." – He is
fled.

XVIII

At home arriving he addressed
His care unto his pistols' plight,
Replaced them in their box, undressed

And Schiller read by candlelight.
But one thought only filled his mind,
His mournful heart no peace could find,
Olga he sees before his eyes
Miraculously fair arise,
Vladimir closes up his book,
And grasps a pen: his verse, albeit
With lovers' rubbish filled, was neat
And flowed harmoniously. He took
And spouted it with lyric fire –
Like D[elvig] when dinner doth inspire.

XIX

Destiny hath preserved his lay.
I have it. Lo! the very thing!
"Oh! whither have ye winged your way,
Ye golden days of my young spring?
What will the coming dawn reveal?
In vain my anxious eyes appeal;
In mist profound all yet is hid.
So be it! Just the laws which bid
The fatal bullet penetrate,

Or innocently past me fly.
Good governs all! The hour draws nigh
Of life or death predestinate.
Blest be the labours of the light,
And blest the shadows of the night.

XX

"To-morrow's dawn will glimmer gray,
Bright day will then begin to burn,
But the dark sepulchre I may
Have entered never to return.
The memory of the bard, a dream,
Will be absorbed by Lethe's stream;
Men will forget me, but my urn
To visit, lovely maid, return,
O'er my remains to drop a tear,
And think: here lies who loved me well,
For consecrate to me he fell
In the dawn of existence drear.
Maid whom my heart desires alone,
Approach, approach; I am thine own."

XXI

Thus in a style **obscure** and **stale**,[64]
He wrote ('tis the romantic style,
Though of romance therein I fail
To see aught – never mind meanwhile)
And about dawn upon his breast
His weary head declined at rest,
For o'er a word to fashion known,
"Ideal," he had drowsy grown.
But scarce had sleep's soft witchery
Subdued him, when his neighbour stept
Into the chamber where he slept
And wakened him with the loud cry:
"'Tis time to get up! Seven doth strike.
Onéguine waits on us, 'tis like."

XXII

He was in error; for Eugene

---

[64] The fact of the above words being italicised suggests the idea that the poet is here firing a Parthian shot at some unfriendly critic.

Was sleeping then a sleep like death;
The pall of night was growing thin,
To Lucifer the cock must breathe
His song, when still he slumbered deep,
The sun had mounted high his steep,
A passing snowstorm wreathed away
With pallid light, but Eugene lay
Upon his couch insensibly;
Slumber still o'er him lingering flies.
But finally he oped his eyes
And turned aside the drapery;
He gazed upon the clock which showed
He long should have been on the road.

XXIII

He rings in haste; in haste arrives
His Frenchman, good Monsieur Guillot,
Who dressing-gown and slippers gives
And linen on him doth bestow.
Dressing as quickly as he can,
Eugene directs the trusty man
To accompany him and to escort

A box of terrible import.
Harnessed the rapid sledge arrived:
He enters: to the mill he drives:
Descends, the order Guillot gives,
The fatal tubes Lepage contrived[65]
To bring behind: the triple steeds
To two young oaks the coachman leads.

XXIV

Lenski the foeman's apparition
Leaning against the dam expects,
Zaretski, village mechanician,
In the meantime the mill inspects.
Onéguine his excuses says;
"But," cried Zaretski in amaze,
"Your second you have left behind!"
A duellist of classic mind,
Method was dear unto his heart
He would not that a man ye slay
In a lax or informal way,

---

65 Lepage – a celebrated gunmaker of former days.

But followed the strict rules of art,
And ancient usages observed
(For which our praise he hath deserved).

XXV

"My second!" cried in turn Eugene,
"Behold my friend Monsieur Guillot;
To this arrangement can be seen,
No obstacle of which I know.
Although unknown to fame mayhap,
He's a straightforward little chap."
Zaretski bit his lip in wrath,
But to Vladimir Eugene saith:
"Shall we commence?" – "Let it be so,"
Lenski replied, and soon they be
Behind the mill. Meantime ye see
Zaretski and Monsieur Guillot
In consultation stand aside –
The foes with downcast eyes abide.

XXVI

Foes! Is it long since friendship rent
Asunder was and hate prepared?
Since leisure was together spent,
Meals, secrets, occupations shared?
Now, like hereditary foes,
Malignant fury they disclose,
As in some frenzied dream of fear
These friends cold-bloodedly draw near
Mutual destruction to contrive.
Cannot they amicably smile
Ere crimson stains their hands defile,
Depart in peace and friendly live?
But fashionable hatred's flame
Trembles at artificial shame.

XXVII

The shining pistols are uncased,
The mallet loud the ramrod strikes,
Bullets are down the barrels pressed,
For the first time the hammer clicks.

Lo! poured in a thin gray cascade,
The powder in the pan is laid,
The sharp flint, screwed securely on,
Is cocked once more. Uneasy grown,
Guillot behind a pollard stood;
Aside the foes their mantles threw,
Zaretski paces thirty-two
Measured with great exactitude.
At each extreme one takes his stand,
A loaded pistol in his hand.

XXVIII

"Advance!" –
  Indifferent and sedate,
The foes, as yet not taking aim,
With measured step and even gait
Athwart the snow four paces came –
Four deadly paces do they span;
Onéguine slowly then began
To raise his pistol to his eye,
Though he advanced unceasingly.
And lo! five paces more they pass,

And Lenski, closing his left eye,
Took aim – but as immediately
Onéguine fired – Alas! alas!
The poet's hour hath sounded – See!
He drops his pistol silently.

XXIX

He on his bosom gently placed
His hand, and fell. His clouded eye
Not agony, but death expressed.
So from the mountain lazily
The avalanche of snow first bends,
Then glittering in the sun descends.
The cold sweat bursting from his brow,
To the youth Eugene hurried now –
Gazed on him, called him. Useless care!
He was no more! The youthful bard
For evermore had disappeared.
The storm was hushed. The blossom fair
Was withered ere the morning light –
The altar flame was quenched in night.

XXX

Tranquil he lay, and strange to view
The peace which on his forehead beamed,
His breast was riddled through and through,
The blood gushed from the wound and steamed
Ere this but one brief moment beat
That heart with inspiration sweet
And enmity and hope and love –
The blood boiled and the passions strove.
Now, as in a deserted house,
All dark and silent hath become;
The inmate is for ever dumb,
The windows whitened, shutters close –
Whither departed is the host?
God knows! The very trace is lost.

XXXI

'Tis sweet the foe to aggravate
With epigrams impertinent,

Sweet to behold him obstinate,
His butting horns in anger bent,
The glass unwittingly inspect
And blush to own himself reflect.
Sweeter it is, my friends, if he
Howl like a dolt: 'tis meant for me!
But sweeter still it is to arrange
For him an honourable grave,
At his pale brow a shot to have,
Placed at the customary range;
But home his body to despatch
Can scarce in sweetness be a match.

XXXII

Well, if your pistol ball by chance
The comrade of your youth should strike,
Who by a haughty word or glance
Or any trifle else ye like
You o'er your wine insulted hath –
Or even overcome by wrath
Scornfully challenged you afield –
Tell me, of sentiments concealed

Which in your spirit dominates,
When motionless your gaze beneath
He lies, upon his forehead death,
And slowly life coagulates –
When deaf and silent he doth lie
Heedless of your despairing cry?

XXXIII

Eugene, his pistol yet in hand
And with remorseful anguish filled,
Gazing on Lenski's corse did stand –
Zaretski shouted: "Why, he's killed!" –
Killed! at this dreadful exclamation
Onéguine went with trepidation
And the attendants called in haste.
Most carefully Zaretski placed
Within his sledge the stiffened corse,
And hurried home his awful freight.
Conscious of death approximate,
Loud paws the earth each panting horse,
His bit with foam besprinkled o'er,
And homeward like an arrow tore.

XXXIV

My friends, the poet ye regret!
When hope's delightful flower but bloomed
In bud of promise incomplete,
The manly toga scarce assumed,
He perished. Where his troubled dreams,
And where the admirable streams
Of youthful impulse, reverie,
Tender and elevated, free?
And where tempestuous love's desires,
The thirst of knowledge and of fame,
Horror of sinfulness and shame,
Imagination's sacred fires,
Ye shadows of a life more high,
Ye dreams of heavenly poesy?

XXXV

Perchance to benefit mankind,
Or but for fame he saw the light;
His lyre, to silence now consigned,
Resounding through all ages might

Have echoed to eternity.
With worldly honours, it may be,
Fortune the poet had repaid.
It may be that his martyred shade
Carried a truth divine away;
That, for the century designed,
Had perished a creative mind,
And past the threshold of decay,
He ne'er shall hear Time's eulogy,
The blessings of humanity.

XXXVI

Or, it may be, the bard had passed
A life in common with the rest;
Vanished his youthful years at last,
The fire extinguished in his breast,
In many things had changed his life –
The Muse abandoned, ta'en a wife,
Inhabited the country, clad
In dressing-gown, a cuckold glad:
A life of fact, not fiction, led –
At forty suffered from the gout,

Eaten, drunk, gossiped and grown stout:
And finally, upon his bed
Had finished life amid his sons,
Doctors and women, sobs and groans.

XXXVII

But, howsoe'er his lot were cast,
Alas! the youthful lover slain,
Poetical enthusiast,
A friendly hand thy life hath ta'en!
There is a spot the village near
Where dwelt the Muses' worshipper,
Two pines have joined their tangled roots,
A rivulet beneath them shoots
Its waters to the neighbouring vale.
There the tired ploughman loves to lie,
The reaping girls approach and ply
Within its wave the sounding pail,
And by that shady rivulet
A simple tombstone hath been set.

XXXVIII

There, when the rains of spring we mark
Upon the meadows showering,
The shepherd plaits his shoe of bark,[66]
Of Volga fishermen doth sing,
And the young damsel from the town,
For summer to the country flown,
Whene'er across the plain at speed
Alone she gallops on her steed,
Stops at the tomb in passing by;
The tightened leathern rein she draws,
Aside she casts her veil of gauze
And reads with rapid eager eye
The simple epitaph – a tear
Doth in her gentle eye appear.

XXXIX

And meditative from the spot

---

[66] In Russia and other northern countries rude shoes are made of the inner bark of the lime tree.

She leisurely away doth ride,
Spite of herself with Lenski's lot
Longtime her mind is occupied.
She muses: "What was Olga's fate?
Longtime was her heart desolate
Or did her tears soon cease to flow?
And where may be her sister now?
Where is the outlaw, banned by men,
Of fashionable dames the foe,
The misanthrope of gloomy brow,
By whom the youthful bard was slain?" –
In time I'll give ye without fail
A true account and in detail.

XL

But not at present, though sincerely
I on my chosen hero dote;
Though I'll return to him right early,
Just at this moment I cannot.
Years have inclined me to stern prose,
Years to light rhyme themselves oppose,
And now, I mournfully confess,

In rhyming I show laziness.
As once, to fill the rapid page
My pen no longer finds delight,
Other and colder thoughts affright,
Sterner solicitudes engage,
In worldly din or solitude
Upon my visions such intrude.

XLI

Fresh aspirations I have known,
I am acquainted with fresh care,
Hopeless are all the first, I own,
Yet still remains the old despair.
Illusions, dream, where, where your
  sweetness?
Where youth (the proper rhyme is
  fleetness)?
And is it true her garland bright
At last is shrunk and withered quite?
And is it true and not a jest,
Not even a poetic phrase,
That vanished are my youthful days

(This joking I used to protest),
Never for me to reappear –
That soon I reach my thirtieth year?

XLII

And so my noon hath come! If so,
I must resign myself, in sooth;
Yet let us part in friendship, O
My frivolous and jolly youth.
I thank thee for thy joyfulness,
Love's tender transports and distress,
For riot, frolics, mighty feeds,
And all that from thy hand proceeds –
I thank thee. In thy company,
With tumult or contentment still
Of thy delights I drank my fill,
Enough! with tranquil spirit I
Commence a new career in life
And rest from bygone days of strife.

XLIII

But pause! Thou calm retreats, farewell,
Where my days in the wilderness
Of languor and of love did tell
And contemplative dreaminess;
And thou, youth's early inspiration,
Invigorate imagination
And spur my spirit's torpid mood!
Fly frequent to my solitude,
Let not the poet's spirit freeze,
Grow harsh and cruel, dead and dry,
Eventually petrify
In the world's mortal revelries,
Amid the soulless sons of pride
And glittering simpletons beside;

XLIV

Amid sly, pusillanimous
Spoiled children most degenerate
And tiresome rogues ridiculous
And stupid censors passionate;

Amid coquettes who pray to God
And abject slaves who kiss the rod;
In haunts of fashion where each day
All with urbanity betray,
Where harsh frivolity proclaims
Its cold unfeeling sentences;
Amid the awful emptiness
Of conversation, thought and aims –
In that morass where you and I
Wallow, my friends, in company!

END OF CANTO THE SIXTH

Canto the Seventh

Moscow

Moscow, Russia's darling daughter,
Where thine equal shall we find?
        Dmitrieff

Who can help loving mother Moscow?
        Baratynski (**Feasts**)

A journey to Moscow! To see the world!
Where better?

Where man is not.
Griboyédoff (**Woe from Wit**)

Canto The Seventh

[Written 1827-1828 at Moscow,
Mikhailovskoe, St. Petersburg
and Malinniki.]

I

Impelled by Spring's dissolving beams,
The snows from off the hills around
Descended swift in turbid streams
And flooded all the level ground.
A smile from slumbering nature clear
Did seem to greet the youthful year;
The heavens shone in deeper blue,
The woods, still naked to the view,
Seemed in a haze of green embowered.
The bee forth from his cell of wax
Flew to collect his rural tax;
The valleys dried and gaily flowered;

Herds low, and under night's dark veil
Already sings the nightingale.

II

Mournful is thine approach to me,
O Spring, thou chosen time of love!
What agitation languidly
My spirit and my blood doth move,
What sad emotions o'er me steal
When first upon my cheek I feel
The breath of Spring again renewed,
Secure in rural quietude –
Or, strange to me is happiness?
Do all things which to mirth incline.
And make a dark existence shine
Inflict annoyance and distress
Upon a soul inert and cloyed? –
And is all light within destroyed?

III

Or, heedless of the leaves' return

Which Autumn late to earth consigned,
Do we alone our losses mourn
Of which the rustling woods remind?
Or, when anew all Nature teems,
Do we foresee in troubled dreams
The coming of life's Autumn drear.
For which no springtime shall appear?
Or, it may be, we inly seek,
Wafted upon poetic wing,
Some other long-departed Spring,
Whose memories make the heart beat
  quick
With thoughts of a far distant land,
Of a strange night when the moon and –

IV

'Tis now the season! Idlers all,
Epicurean philosophers,
Ye men of fashion cynical,
Of Levshin's school ye followers,[67]

---

[67] Levshin – a contemporary writer on political economy.

Priams of country populations
And dames of fine organisations,
Spring summons you to her green
  bowers,
'Tis the warm time of labour, flowers;
The time for mystic strolls which late
Into the starry night extend.
Quick to the country let us wend
In vehicles surcharged with freight;
In coach or post-cart duly placed
Beyond the city-barriers haste.

V

Thou also, reader generous,
The chaise long ordered please employ,
Abandon cities riotous,
Which in the winter were a joy:
The Muse capricious let us coax,
Go hear the rustling of the oaks
Beside a nameless rivulet,
Where in the country Eugene yet,
An idle anchorite and sad,

A while ago the winter spent,
Near young Tattiana resident,
My pretty self-deceiving maid –
No more the village knows his face,
For there he left a mournful trace.

VI

Let us proceed unto a rill,
Which in a hilly neighbourhood
Seeks, winding amid meadows still,
The river through the linden wood.
The nightingale there all night long,
Spring's paramour, pours forth her song
The fountain brawls, sweetbriers bloom,
And lo! where lies a marble tomb
And two old pines their branches
  spread –
"**Vladimir Lenski lies beneath,**
Who early died a gallant death,"
Thereon the passing traveller read:
"**The date, his fleeting years how**
  long –

Repose in peace, thou child of song."

VII

Time was, the breath of early dawn
Would agitate a mystic wreath
Hung on a pine branch earthward drawn
Above the humble urn of death.
Time was, two maidens from their home
At eventide would hither come,
And, by the light the moonbeams gave,
Lament, embrace upon that grave.
But now – none heeds the monument
Of woe: effaced the pathway now:
There is no wreath upon the bough:
Alone beside it, gray and bent,
As formerly the shepherd sits
And his poor basten sandal knits.

VIII

My poor Vladimir, bitter tears

Thee but a little space bewept,
Faithless, alas! thy maid appears,
Nor true unto her sorrow kept.
Another could her heart engage,
Another could her woe assuage
By flattery and lover's art –
A lancer captivates her heart!
A lancer her soul dotes upon:
Before the altar, lo! the pair,
Mark ye with what a modest air
She bows her head beneath the crown;[68]
Behold her downcast eyes which glow,
Her lips where light smiles come and go!

IX

My poor Vladimir! In the tomb,
Passed into dull eternity,
Was the sad poet filled with gloom,
Hearing the fatal perfidy?

---

[68] The crown used in celebrating marriages in Russia according to the forms of the Eastern Church. See Note 28.

Or, beyond Lethe lulled to rest,
Hath the bard, by indifference blest,
Callous to all on earth become –
Is the world to him sealed and dumb?
The same unmoved oblivion
On us beyond the grave attends,
The voice of lovers, foes and friends,
Dies suddenly: of heirs alone
Remains on earth the unseemly rage,
Whilst struggling for the heritage.

X

Soon Olga's accents shrill resound
No longer through her former home;
The lancer, to his calling bound,
Back to his regiment must roam.
The aged mother, bathed in tears,
Distracted by her grief appears
When the hour came to bid good-bye –
But my Tattiana's eyes were dry.
Only her countenance assumed
A deadly pallor, air distressed;

When all around the entrance pressed,
To say farewell, and fussed and fumed
Around the carriage of the pair –
Tattiana gently led them there.

XI

And long her eyes as through a haze
After the wedded couple strain;
Alas! the friend of childish days
Away, Tattiana, hath been ta'en.
Thy dove, thy darling little pet
On whom a sister's heart was set
Afar is borne by cruel fate,
For evermore is separate.
She wanders aimless as a sprite,
Into the tangled garden goes
But nowhere can she find repose,
Nor even tears afford respite,
Of consolation all bereft –
Well nigh her heart in twain was cleft.

XII

In cruel solitude each day
With flame more ardent passion burns,
And to Onéguine far away
Her heart importunately turns.
She never more his face may view,
For was it not her duty to
Detest him for a brother slain?
The poet fell; already men
No more remembered him; unto
Another his betrothed was given;
The memory of the bard was driven
Like smoke athwart the heaven blue;
Two hearts perchance were desolate
And mourned him still. Why mourn his
 fate?

XIII

'Twas eve. 'Twas dusk. The river speeds
In tranquil flow. The beetle hums.

Already dance to song proceeds;
The fisher's fire afar illumes
The river's bank. Tattiana lone
Beneath the silver of the moon
Long time in meditation deep
Her path across the plain doth keep –
Proceeds, until she from a hill
Sees where a noble mansion stood,
A village and beneath, a wood,
A garden by a shining rill.
She gazed thereon, and instant beat
Her heart more loudly and more fleet.

XIV

She hesitates, in doubt is thrown –
"Shall I proceed, or homeward flee?
He is not there: I am not known:
The house and garden I would see."
Tattiana from the hill descends
With bated breath, around she bends
A countenance perplexed and scared.
She enters a deserted yard –

Yelping, a pack of dogs rush out,
But at her shriek ran forth with noise
The household troop of little boys,
Who with a scuffle and a shout
The curs away to kennel chase,
The damsel under escort place.

XV

"Can I inspect the mansion, please?"
Tattiana asks, and hurriedly
Unto Anicia for the keys
The family of children hie.
Anicia soon appears, the door
Opens unto her visitor.
Into the lonely house she went,
Wherein a space Onéguine spent.
She gazed – a cue, forgotten long,
Doth on the billiard table rest,
Upon the tumbled sofa placed,
A riding whip. She strolls along.
The beldam saith: "The hearth, by it
The master always used to sit.

XVI

"Departed Lenski here to dine
In winter time would often come.
Please follow this way, lady mine,
This is my master's sitting-room.
'Tis here he slept, his coffee took,
Into accounts would sometimes look,
A book at early morn perused.
The room my former master used.
On Sundays by yon window he,
Spectacles upon nose, all day
Was wont with me at cards to play.
God save his soul eternally
And grant his weary bones their rest
Deep in our mother Earth's chill breast!"

XVII

Tattiana's eyes with tender gleam
On everything around her gaze,
Of priceless value all things seem
And in her languid bosom raise

A pleasure though with sorrow knit:
The table with its lamp unlit,
The pile of books, with carpet spread
Beneath the window-sill his bed,
The landscape which the moonbeams
  fret,
The twilight pale which softens all,
Lord Byron's portrait on the wall
And the cast-iron statuette
With folded arms and eyes bent low,
Cocked hat and melancholy brow.[69]

XVIII

Long in this fashionable cell
Tattiana as enchanted stood;
But it grew late; cold blew the gale;
Dark was the valley and the wood
Slept o'er the river misty grown.
Behind the mountain sank the moon.
Long, long the hour had past when home

[69] The Russians not unfrequently adorn their apartments with effigies of the great Napoleon.

Our youthful wanderer should roam.
She hid the trouble of her breast,
Heaved an involuntary sigh
And turned to leave immediately,
But first permission did request
Thither in future to proceed
That certain volumes she might read.

XIX

Adieu she to the matron said
At the front gates, but in brief space
At early morn returns the maid
To the abandoned dwelling-place.
When in the study's calm retreat,
Wrapt in oblivion complete,
She found herself alone at last,
Longtime her tears flowed thick and fast;
But presently she tried to read;
At first for books was disinclined,
But soon their choice seemed to her mind

Remarkable. She then indeed
Devoured them with an eager zest.
A new world was made manifest!

XX

Although we know that Eugene had
Long ceased to be a reading man,
Still certain authors, I may add,
He had excepted from the ban:
The bard of Juan and the Giaour,
With it may be a couple more;
Romances three, in which ye scan
Portrayed contemporary man
As the reflection of his age,
His immorality of mind
To arid selfishness resigned,
A visionary personage
With his exasperated sense,
His energy and impotence.

XXI

And numerous pages had preserved
The sharp incisions of his nail,
And these the attentive maid observed
With eye precise and without fail.
Tattiana saw with trepidation
By what idea or observation
Onéguine was the most impressed,
In what he merely acquiesced.
Upon those margins she perceived
Onéguine's pencillings. His mind
Made revelations undesigned,
Of what he thought and what believed,
A dagger, asterisk, or note
Interrogation to denote.

XXII

And my Tattiana now began
To understand by slow degrees
More clearly, God be praised, the man,
Whom autocratic fate's decrees

Had bid her sigh for without hope –
A dangerous, gloomy misanthrope,
Being from hell or heaven sent,
Angel or fiend malevolent.
Which is he? or an imitation,
A bogy conjured up in joke,
A Russian in Childe Harold's cloak,
Of foreign whims the impersonation –
Handbook of fashionable phrase
Or parody of modern ways?

XXIII

Hath she found out the riddle yet?
Hath she a fitting phrase selected?
But time flies and she doth forget
They long at home have her expected –
Whither two neighbouring dames have
  walked
And a long time about her talked.
"What can be done? She is no child!"
Cried the old dame with anguish filled:
"Olinka is her junior, see.

'Tis time to marry her, 'tis true,
But tell me what am I to do?
To all she answers cruelly –
I will not wed, and ever weeps
And lonely through the forest creeps."

XXIV

"Is she in love?" quoth one. "With whom?
Bouyànoff courted. She refused.
Pétòushkoff met the selfsame doom.
The hussar Pykhtin was accused.
How the young imp on Tania doted!
To captivate her how devoted!
I mused: perhaps the matter's
squared –
O yes! my hopes soon disappeared."
"But, **mátushka**, to Moscow you[70]
Should go, the market for a maid,
With many a vacancy, 'tis said." –

---

70 "Mátushka," or "little mother," a term of endearment in constant use amongst Russian females.

"Alas! my friend, no revenue!"
"Enough to see one winter's end;
If not, the money I will lend."

XXV

The venerable dame opined
The counsel good and full of reason,
Her money counted, and designed
To visit Moscow in the season.
Tattiana learns the intelligence –
Of her provincial innocence
The unaffected traits she now
Unto a carping world must show –
Her toilette's antiquated style,
Her antiquated mode of speech,
For Moscow fops and Circes each
To mark with a contemptuous smile.
Horror! had she not better stay
Deep in the greenwood far away?

XXVI

Arising with the morning's light,
Unto the fields she makes her way,
And with emotional delight
Surveying them, she thus doth say:
"Ye peaceful valleys all, good-bye!
Ye well-known mountain summits high,
Ye groves whose depths I know so well,
Thou beauteous sky above, farewell!
Delicious nature, thee I fly,
The calm existence which I prize
I yield for splendid vanities,
Thou too farewell, my liberty!
Whither and wherefore do I speed
And what will Destiny concede?"

XXVII

Farther Tattiana's walks extend –
'Tis now the hillock now the rill
Their natural attractions lend
To stay the maid against her will.

She the acquaintances she loves,
Her spacious fields and shady groves,
Another visit hastes to pay.
But Summer swiftly fades away
And golden Autumn draweth nigh,
And pallid nature trembling grieves,
A victim decked with golden leaves;
Dark clouds before the north wind fly;
It blew: it howled: till winter e'en
Came forth in all her magic sheen.

XXVIII

The snow descends and buries all,
Hangs heavy on the oaken boughs,
A white and undulating pall
O'er hillock and o'er meadow throws.
The channel of the river stilled
As if with eider-down is filled.
The hoar-frost glitters: all rejoice
In mother Winter's strange caprice.
But Tania's heart is not at ease,
Winter's approach she doth not hail

Nor the frost particles inhale
Nor the first snow of winter seize
Her shoulders, breast and face to lave –
Alarm the winter journey gave.

XXIX

The date was fixed though oft postponed,
But ultimately doth approach.
Examined, mended, newly found
Was the old and forgotten coach;
Kibitkas three, the accustomed train,[71]
The household property contain:

---

[71] In former times, and to some extent the practice still continues to the present day, Russian families were wont to travel with every necessary of life, and, in the case of the wealthy, all its luxuries following in their train. As the poet complains in a subsequent stanza there were no inns; and if the simple Làrinas required such ample store of creature comforts the impediments accompanying a great noble on his journeys may be easily conceived.

Saucepans and mattresses and chairs,
Portmanteaus and preserves in jars,
Feather-beds, also poultry-coops,
Basins and jugs – well! everything
To happiness contributing.
Behold! beside their dwelling groups
Of serfs the farewell wail have given.
Nags eighteen to the door are driven.

XXX

These to the coach of state are bound,
Breakfast the busy cooks prepare,
Baggage is heaped up in a mound,
Old women at the coachmen swear.
A bearded postillion astride
A lean and shaggy nag doth ride,
Unto the gates the servants fly
To bid the gentlefolk good-bye.
These take their seats; the coach of state
Leisurely through the gateway glides.
"Adieu! thou home where peace abides,
Where turmoil cannot penetrate,

Shall I behold thee once again?" –
Tattiana tears cannot restrain.

XXXI

The limits of enlightenment
When to enlarge we shall succeed,
In course of time (the whole extent
Will not five centuries exceed
By computation) it is like
Our roads transformed the eye will strike;
Highways all Russia will unite
And form a network left and right;
On iron bridges we shall gaze
Which o'er the waters boldly leap,
Mountains we'll level and through deep
Streams excavate subaqueous ways,
And Christian folk will, I expect,
An inn at every stage erect.

XXXII

But now, what wretched roads one sees,

Our bridges long neglected rot,
And at the stages bugs and fleas
One moment's slumber suffer not.
Inns there are none. Pretentious but
Meagre, within a draughty hut,
A bill of fare hangs full in sight
And irritates the appetite.
Meantime a Cyclops of those parts
Before a fire which feebly glows
Mends with the Russian hammer's blows
The flimsy wares of Western marts,
With blessings on the ditches and
The ruts of his own fatherland.

XXXIII

Yet on a frosty winter day
The journey in a sledge doth please,
No senseless fashionable lay
Glides with a more luxurious ease;
For our Automedons are fire
And our swift troikas never tire;
The verst posts catch the vacant eye

And like a palisade flit by.[72]
The Làrinas unwisely went,
From apprehension of the cost,
By their own horses, not the post –
So Tania to her heart's content
Could taste the pleasures of the road.
Seven days and nights the travellers
  plod.

XXXIV

But they draw near. Before them, lo!

---

[72] This somewhat musty joke has appeared in more than one national costume. Most Englishmen, if we were to replace verst-posts with milestones and substitute a graveyard for a palisade, would instantly recognize its Yankee extraction. In Russia however its origin is as ancient at least as the reign of Catherine the Second. The witticism ran thus: A courier sent by Prince Potemkin to the Empress drove so fast that his sword, projecting from the vehicle, rattled against the verst-posts as if against a palisade!]

White Moscow raises her old spires,
Whose countless golden crosses glow
As with innumerable fires.[73]
Ah! brethren, what was my delight
When I yon semicircle bright
Of churches, gardens, belfries high
Descried before me suddenly!
Moscow, how oft in evil days,
Condemned to exile dire by fate,
On thee I used to meditate!

---

[73] The aspect of Moscow, especially as seen from the Sparrow Hills, a low range bordering the river Moskva at a short distance from the city, is unique and splendid. It possesses several domes completely plated with gold and some twelve hundred spires most of which are surmounted by a golden cross. At the time of sunset they seem literally tipped with flame. It was from this memorable spot that Napoleon and the Grand Army first obtained a glimpse at the city of the Tsars. There are three hundred and seventy churches in Moscow. The Kremlin itself is however by far the most interesting object to the stranger.

Moscow! How much is in the phrase
For every loyal Russian breast!
How much is in that word expressed!

XXXV

Lo! compassed by his grove of oaks,
Petrovski Palace! Gloomily
His recent glory he invokes.
Here, drunk with his late victory,
Napoleon tarried till it please
Moscow approach on bended knees,
Time-honoured Kremlin's keys present.
Not so! My Moscow never went
To seek him out with bended head.
No gift she bears, no feast proclaims,
But lights incendiary flames
For the impatient chief instead.
From hence engrossed in thought
  profound
He on the conflagration frowned.[74]

---

[74] Napoleon on his arrival in Moscow on the 14th September took up his quarters in the

XXXVI

Adieu, thou witness of our glory,
Petrovski Palace; come, astir!
Drive on! the city barriers hoary
Appear; along the road of Tver
The coach is borne o'er ruts and holes,
Past women, sentry-boxes, rolls,
Past palaces and nunneries,

Kremlin, but on the 16th had to remove to the Petrovski Palace or Castle on account of the conflagration which broke out in all quarters of the city. He however returned to the Kremlin on the 19th September. The Palace itself is placed in the midst of extensive grounds just outside the city, on the road to Tver, i.e. to the northwest. It is perhaps worthy of remark, as one amongst numerous circumstances proving how extensively the poet interwove his own life-experiences with the plot of this poem, that it was by this road that he himself must have been in the habit of approaching Moscow from his favourite country residence of Mikhailovskoe, in the province of Pskoff.

Lamp-posts, shops, sledges, families,
Bokharians, peasants, beds of greens,
Boulevards, belfries, milliners,
Huts, chemists, Cossacks, shopkeepers
And fashionable magazines,
Balconies, lion's heads on doors,
Jackdaws on every spire – in scores.[75]

XXXVII

The weary way still incomplete,
An hour passed by – another – till,
Near Khariton's in a side street
The coach before a house stood still.
At an old aunt's they had arrived
Who had for four long years survived
An invalid from lung complaint.
A Kalmuck gray, in caftan rent

---

[75] The first line refers to the prevailing shape of the cast-iron handles which adorn the porte cochères. The Russians are fond of tame birds – jackdaws, pigeons, starlings, etc., abound in Moscow and elsewhere.

And spectacles, his knitting staid
And the saloon threw open wide;
The princess from the sofa cried
And the newcomers welcome bade.
The two old ladies then embraced
And exclamations interlaced.

XXXVIII

"Princesse, mon ange!" – "Pachette!" –
"Aline!"
"Who would have thought it? As of yore!
Is it for long?" – "Ma chère cousine!"
"Sit down. How funny, to be sure!
'Tis a scene of romance, I vow!"
"Tania, my eldest child, you know" –
"Ah! come, Tattiana, come to me!
Is it a dream, and can it be?
Cousin, rememb'rest Grandison?"
"What! Grandison?" – "Yes, certainly!"
"Oh! I remember, where is he?" –
"Here, he resides with Simeon.
He called upon me Christmas Eve –

His son is married, just conceive!"

XXXIX

"And he – but of him presently –
To-morrow Tania we will show,
What say you? to the family –
Alas! abroad I cannot go.
See, I can hardly crawl about –
But you must both be quite tired out!
Let us go seek a little rest –
Ah! I'm so weak – my throbbing breast!
Oppressive now is happiness,
Not only sorrow – Ah! my dear,
Now I am fit for nothing here.
In old age life is weariness!"
Then weeping she sank back distressed
And fits of coughing racked her chest.

XL

By the sick lady's gaiety
And kindness Tania was impressed,

But, her own room in memory,
The strange apartment her oppressed:
Repose her silken curtains fled,
She could not sleep in her new bed.
The early tinkling of the bells
Which of approaching labour tells
Aroused Tattiana from her bed.
The maiden at her casement sits
As daylight glimmers, darkness flits,
But ah! discerns nor wood nor mead –
Beneath her lay a strange courtyard,
A stable, kitchen, fence appeared.

XLI

To consanguineous dinners they
Conduct Tattiana constantly,
That grandmothers and grandsires may
Contemplate her sad reverie.
We Russians, friends from distant parts
Ever receive with kindly hearts
And exclamations and good cheer.
"How Tania grows! Doth it appear

Long since I held thee at the font –
Since in these arms I thee did bear –
And since I pulled thee by the ear –
And I to give thee cakes was wont?" –
Then the old dames in chorus sing,
"Oh! how our years are vanishing!"

XLII

But nothing changed in them is seen,
All in the good old style appears,
Our dear old aunt, Princess Helène,
Her cap of tulle still ever wears:
Luceria Lvovna paint applies,
Amy Petrovna utters lies,
Ivan Petròvitch still a gaby,
Simeon Petròvitch just as shabby;
Pélagie Nikolavna has
Her friend Monsieur Finemouche the
  same,
Her wolf-dog and her husband tame;
Still of his club he member was –
As deaf and silly doth remain,

Still eats and drinks enough for twain.

XLIII

Their daughters kiss Tattiana fair.
In the beginning, cold and mute,
Moscow's young Graces at her stare,
Examine her from head to foot.
They deem her somewhat finical,
Outlandish and provincial,
A trifle pale, a trifle lean,
But plainer girls they oft had seen.
Obedient then to Nature's law,
With her they did associate,
Squeeze tiny hands and osculate;
Her tresses curled in fashion saw,
And oft in whispers would impart
A maiden's secrets – of the heart.

XLIV

Triumphs – their own or those of
friends –

Hopes, frolics, dreams and sentiment
Their harmless conversation blends
With scandal's trivial ornament.
Then to reward such confidence
Her amorous experience
With mute appeal to ask they seem –
But Tania just as in a dream
Without participation hears,
Their voices nought to her impart
And the lone secret of her heart,
Her sacred hoard of joy and tears,
She buries deep within her breast
Nor aught confides unto the rest.

XLV

Tattiana would have gladly heard
The converse of the world polite,
But in the drawing-room all appeared
To find in gossip such delight,
Speech was so tame and colourless
Their slander e'en was weariness;
In their sterility of prattle,

Questions and news and tittle-tattle,
No sense was ever manifest
Though by an error and unsought –
The languid mind could smile at nought,
Heart would not throb albeit in jest –
Even amusing fools we miss
In thee, thou world of empty bliss.

XLVI

In groups, official striplings glance
Conceitedly on Tania fair,
And views amongst themselves advance
Unfavourable unto her.
But one buffoon unhappy deemed
Her the ideal which he dreamed,
And leaning 'gainst the portal closed
To her an elegy composed.
Also one Viázemski, remarking
Tattiana by a poor aunt's side,
Successfully to please her tried,
And an old gent the poet marking

By Tania, smoothing his peruke,
To ask her name the trouble took.[76]

XLVII

But where Melpomene doth rave
With lengthened howl and accent loud,
And her bespangled robe doth wave
Before a cold indifferent crowd,
And where Thalia softly dreams
And heedless of approval seems,
Terpsichore alone among
Her sisterhood delights the young
(So 'twas with us in former years,
In your young days and also mine),
Never upon my heroine

---

[76] One of the obscure satirical allusions contained in this poem. Doubtless the joke was perfectly intelligible to the habitués of contemporary St. Petersburg society. Viazemski of course is the poet and prince, Pushkin's friend.

The jealous dame her lorgnette veers,
The connoisseur his glances throws
From boxes or from stalls in rows.

XLVIII

To the assembly her they bear.
There the confusion, pressure, heat,
The crash of music, candles' glare
And rapid whirl of many feet,
The ladies' dresses airy, light,
The motley moving mass and bright,
Young ladies in a vasty curve,
To strike imagination serve.
'Tis there that arrant fops display
Their insolence and waistcoats white
And glasses unemployed all night;
Thither hussars on leave will stray
To clank the spur, delight the fair –
And vanish like a bird in air.

XLIX

Full many a lovely star hath night
And Moscow many a beauty fair:
Yet clearer shines than every light
The moon in the blue atmosphere.
And she to whom my lyre would fain,
Yet dares not, dedicate its strain,
Shines in the female firmament
Like a full moon magnificent.
Lo! with what pride celestial
Her feet the earth beneath her press!
Her heart how full of gentleness,
Her glance how wild yet genial!
Enough, enough, conclude thy lay –
For folly's dues thou hadst to pay.

L

Noise, laughter, bowing, hurrying mixt,
Gallop, mazurka, waltzing – see!
A pillar by, two aunts betwixt,
Tania, observed by nobody,

Looks upon all with absent gaze
And hates the world's discordant ways.

'Tis noisome to her there: in thought
Again her rural life she sought,
The hamlet, the poor villagers,
The little solitary nook
Where shining runs the tiny brook,
Her garden, and those books of hers,
And the lime alley's twilight dim
Where the first time she met with **him**.

LI

Thus widely meditation erred,
Forgot the world, the noisy ball,
Whilst from her countenance ne'er stirred
The eyes of a grave general.
Both aunts looked knowing as a judge,
Each gave Tattiana's arm a nudge
And in a whisper did repeat:

"Look quickly to your left, my sweet!"
"The left? Why, what on earth is
  there?" –
"No matter, look immediately.
There, in that knot of company,
Two dressed in uniform appear –
Ah! he has gone the other way" –
"Who? Is it that stout general, pray?" –

LII

Let us congratulations pay
To our Tattiana conquering,
And for a time our course delay,
That I forget not whom I sing.
Let me explain that in my song
"I celebrate a comrade young
And the extent of his caprice;
O epic Muse, my powers increase
And grant success to labour long;
Having a trusty staff bestowed,

Grant that I err not on the road."
Enough! my pack is now unslung –
To classicism I've homage paid,
Though late, have a beginning made.[77]

END OF CANTO THE SEVENTH

---

[77] Many will consider this mode of bringing the canto to a conclusion of more than doubtful taste. The poet evidently aims a stroke at the pedantic and narrow-minded criticism to which original genius, emancipated from the strait-waistcoat of conventionality, is not unfrequently subjected.

Canto the Eighth

The Great World

‘Fare thee well, and if for ever,
Still for ever fare thee well.’ – Byron
Canto the Eighth

[St. Petersburg, Boldino, Tsarskoe Selo, 1880-1881]

I

In the Lyceum's noiseless shade
As in a garden when I grew,
I Apuleius gladly read
But would not look at Cicero.
'Twas then in valleys lone, remote,
In spring-time, heard the cygnet's note
By waters shining tranquilly,
That first the Muse appeared to me.
Into the study of the boy
There came a sudden flash of light,
The Muse revealed her first delight,
Sang childhood's pastimes and its joy,
Glory with which our history teems
And the heart's agitated dreams.

II

And the world met her smilingly,
A first success light pinions gave,
The old Derjavine noticed me,

And blest me, sinking to the grave.[78]
Then my companions young with
  pleasure
In the unfettered hours of leisure
Her utterances ever heard,

---

[78] This touching scene produced a lasting impression on Pushkin's mind. It took place at a public examination at the Lyceum, on which occasion the boy poet produced a poem. The incident recalls the "Mon cher Tibulle" of Voltaire and the youthful Parny (see Note 42). Derjavine flourished during the reigns of Catherine the Second and Alexander the First. His poems are stiff and formal in style and are not much thought of by contemporary Russians. But a century back a very infinitesimal endowment of literary ability was sufficient to secure imperial reward and protection, owing to the backward state of the empire. Stanza II properly concludes with this line, the remainder having been expunged either by the author himself or the censors. I have filled up the void with lines from a fragment left by the author having reference to this canto.

And by a partial temper stirred
And boiling o'er with friendly heat,
They first of all my brow did wreathe
And an encouragement did breathe
That my coy Muse might sing more
  sweet.
O triumphs of my guileless days,
How sweet a dream your memories raise!

III

Passion's wild sway I then allowed,
Her promptings unto law did make,
Pursuits I followed of the crowd,
My sportive Muse I used to take
To many a noisy feast and fight,
Terror of guardians of the night;
And wild festivities among
She brought with her the gift of song.
Like a Bacchante in her sport
Beside the cup she sang her rhymes
And the young revellers of past times
Vociferously paid her court,

And I, amid the friendly crowd,
Of my light paramour was proud.

IV

But I abandoned their array,
And fled afar – she followed me.
How oft the kindly Muse away
Hath whiled the road's monotony,
Entranced me by some mystic tale.
How oft beneath the moonbeams pale
Like Leonora did she ride[79]
With me Caucasian rocks beside!
How oft to the Crimean shore
She led me through nocturnal mist
Unto the sounding sea to list,
Where Nereids murmur evermore,
And where the billows hoarsely raise
To God eternal hymns of praise.

---

[79] See Note 30, "Leonora," a poem by Gottfried Augustus Burger, b. 1748, d. 1794.

V

Then, the far capital forgot,
Its splendour and its blandishments,
In poor Moldavia cast her lot,
She visited the humble tents
Of migratory gipsy hordes –
And wild among them grew her words –
Our godlike tongue she could exchange
For savage speech, uncouth and
  strange,
And ditties of the steppe she loved.
But suddenly all changed around!
Lo! in my garden was she found
And as a country damsel roved,
A pensive sorrow in her glance
And in her hand a French romance.

VI

Now for the first time I my Muse
Lead into good society,
Her steppe-like beauties I peruse

With jealous fear, anxiety.
Through dense aristocratic rows
Of diplomats and warlike beaux
And supercilious dames she glides,
Sits down and gazes on all sides –
Amazed at the confusing crowd,
Variety of speech and vests,
Deliberate approach of guests
Who to the youthful hostess bowed,
And the dark fringe of men, like frames
Enclosing pictures of fair dames.

VII

Assemblies oligarchical
Please her by their decorum fixed,
The rigour of cold pride and all
Titles and ages intermixed.
But who in that choice company
With clouded brow stands silently?
Unknown to all he doth appear,
A vision desolate and drear
Doth seem to him the festal scene.

Doth his brow wretchedness declare
Or suffering pride? Why is he there?
Who may he be? Is it Eugene?
Pray is it he? It is the same.
"And is it long since back he came?

VIII

"Is he the same or grown more wise?
Still doth the misanthrope appear?
He has returned, say in what guise?
What is his latest character?
What doth he act? Is it Melmoth,[80]
Philanthropist or patriot,
Childe Harold, quaker, devotee,
Or other mask donned playfully?
Or a good fellow for the nonce,
Like you and me and all the rest? –
But this is my advice, 'twere best
Not to behave as he did once –

---

80 A romance by Maturin.

Society he duped enow."
"Is he known to you?" – "Yes and No."

IX

Wherefore regarding him express
Perverse, unfavourable views?
Is it that human restlessness
For ever carps, condemns, pursues?
Is it that ardent souls of flame
By recklessness amuse or shame
Selfish nonentities around?
That mind which yearns for space is
 bound?
And that too often we receive
Professions eagerly for deeds,
That crass stupidity misleads,
That we by cant ourselves deceive,
That mediocrity alone
Without disgust we look upon?

X

Happy he who in youth was young,
Happy who timely grew mature,
He who life's frosts which early wrung
Hath gradually learnt to endure;
By visions who was ne'er deranged
Nor from the mob polite estranged,
At twenty who was prig or swell,
At thirty who was married well,
At fifty who relief obtained
From public and from private ties,
Who glory, wealth and dignities
Hath tranquilly in turn attained,
And unto whom we all allude
As to a worthy man and good!

XI

But sad is the reflection made,
In vain was youth by us received,
That we her constantly betrayed
And she at last hath us deceived;

That our desires which noblest seemed,
The purest of the dreams we dreamed,
Have one by one all withered grown
Like rotten leaves by Autumn strown –
'Tis fearful to anticipate
Nought but of dinners a long row,
To look on life as on a show,
Eternally to imitate
The seemly crowd, partaking nought
Its passions and its modes of thought.

XII

The butt of scandal having been,
'Tis dreadful – ye agree, I hope –
To pass with reasonable men
For a fictitious misanthrope,
A visionary mortified,
Or monster of Satanic pride,
Or e'en the "Demon" of my strain.[81]

---

[81] The "Demon," a short poem by Pushkin which at its first appearance created some excitement in Russian society. A more

Onéguine – take him up again –
In duel having killed his friend
And reached, with nought his mind to
  engage,
The twenty-sixth year of his age,
Wearied of leisure in the end,
Without profession, business, wife,
He knew not how to spend his life.

XIII

Him a disquietude did seize,
A wish from place to place to roam,

---

appropriate, or at any rate explanatory title, would have been the Tempter. It is descriptive of the first manifestation of doubt and cynicism in his youthful mind, allegorically as the visits of a "demon." Russian society was moved to embody this imaginary demon in the person of a certain friend of Pushkin's. This must not be confounded with Lermontoff's poem bearing the same title upon which Rubinstein's new opera, "Il Demonio," is founded.

A very troublesome disease,
In some a willing martyrdom.
Abandoned he his country seat,
Of woods and fields the calm retreat,
Where every day before his eyes
A blood-bespattered shade would rise,
And aimless journeys did commence –
But still remembrance to him clings,
His travels like all other things
Inspired but weariness intense;
Returning, from his ship amid
A ball he fell as Tchatzki did.[82]

XIV

Behold, the crowd begins to stir,
A whisper runs along the hall,
A lady draws the hostess near,
Behind her a grave general.
Her manners were deliberate,

---

82 Tchatzki, one of the principal characters in Griboyédoff's celebrated comedy "Woe from Wit" (Gore ot Ouma).

Reserved, but not inanimate,
Her eyes no saucy glance address,
There was no angling for success.
Her features no grimaces bleared;
Of affectation innocent,
Calm and without embarrassment,
A faithful model she appeared
Of “comme il faut.” Shishkòff, forgive!
I can’t translate the adjective.[83]

XV

Ladies in crowds around her close,
Her with a smile old women greet,
The men salute with lower bows
And watch her eye’s full glance to meet.
Maidens before her meekly move

---

[83] Shishkòff was a member of the literary school which cultivated the vernacular as opposed to the Arzamass or Gallic school, to which the poet himself and his uncle Vassili Pushkin belonged. He was admiral, author, and minister of education.

Along the hall, and high above
The crowd doth head and shoulders rise
The general who accompanies.
None could her beautiful declare,
Yet viewing her from head to foot,
None could a trace of that impute,
Which in the elevated sphere
Of London life is "vulgar" called
And ruthless fashion hath blackballed.

XVI

I like this word exceedingly
Although it will not bear translation,
With us 'tis quite a novelty
Not high in general estimation;
'Twould serve ye in an epigram –
But turn we once more to our dame.
Enchanting, but unwittingly,
At table she was sitting by
The brilliant Nina Voronskoi,
The Neva's Cleopatra, and
None the conviction could withstand

That Nina's marble symmetry,
Though dazzling its effulgence white,
Could not eclipse her neighbour's light.

XVII

"And is it," meditates Eugene.
"And is it she? It must be – no –
How! from the waste of steppes
  unseen," –
And the eternal lorgnette through
Frequent and rapid doth his glance
Seek the forgotten countenance
Familiar to him long ago.
"Inform me, prince, pray dost thou know
The lady in the crimson cap
Who with the Spanish envoy speaks?" –
The prince's eye Onéguine seeks:
"Ah! long the world hath missed thy
  shape!
But stop! I will present thee, if
You choose." – "But who is she?" – "My
  wife."

XVIII

"So thou art wed! I did not know.
Long ago?" – "'Tis the second year."
"To – ?" – "Làrina." – "Tattiana?" – "So.
And dost thou know her?" – "We live
near."
"Then come with me." The prince
proceeds,
His wife approaches, with him leads
His relative and friend as well.
The lady's glance upon him fell –
And though her soul might be confused,
And vehemently though amazed
She on the apparition gazed,
No signs of trouble her accused,
A mien unaltered she preserved,
Her bow was easy, unreserved.

XIX

Ah no! no faintness her attacked
Nor sudden turned she red or white,

Her brow she did not e'en contract
Nor yet her lip compressed did bite.
Though he surveyed her at his ease,
Not the least trace Onéguine sees
Of the Tattiana of times fled.
He conversation would have led –
But could not. Then she questioned
 him: –
"Had he been long here, and where
 from?
Straight from their province had he
 come?" –
Cast upwards then her eyeballs dim
Unto her husband, went away –
Transfixed Onéguine mine doth stay.

XX

Is this the same Tattiana, say,
Before whom once in solitude,
In the beginning of this lay,
Deep in the distant province rude,
Impelled by zeal for moral worth,

He salutary rules poured forth?
The maid whose note he still possessed
Wherein the heart its vows expressed,
Where all upon the surface lies, –
That girl – but he must dreaming be –
That girl whom once on a time he
Could in a humble sphere despise,
Can she have been a moment gone
Thus haughty, careless in her tone?

XXI

He quits the fashionable throng
And meditative homeward goes,
Visions, now sad, now grateful, long
Do agitate his late repose.
He wakes – they with a letter come –
The Princess N. will be at home
On such a day. O Heavens, 'tis she!
Oh! I accept. And instantly
He a polite reply doth scrawl.
What hath he dreamed? What hath
  occurred?

In the recesses what hath stirred
Of a heart cold and cynical?
Vexation? Vanity? or strove
Again the plague of boyhood – love?

XXII

The hours once more Onéguine counts,
Impatient waits the close of day,
But ten strikes and his sledge he mounts
And gallops to her house away.
Trembling he seeks the young
  princess –
Tattiana finds in loneliness.
Together moments one or two
They sat, but conversation's flow
Deserted Eugene. He, distraught,
Sits by her gloomily, desponds,
Scarce to her questions he responds,
Full of exasperating thought.
He fixedly upon her stares –
She calm and unconcerned appears.

XXIII

The husband comes and interferes
With this unpleasant **tête-à-tête**,
With Eugene pranks of former years
And jests doth recapitulate.
They talked and laughed. The guests arrived.
The conversation was revived
By the coarse wit of worldly hate;
But round the hostess scintillate
Light sallies without coxcombry,
Awhile sound conversation seems
To banish far unworthy themes
And platitudes and pedantry,
And never was the ear affright
By liberties or loose or light.

XXIV

And yet the city's flower was there,
Noblesse and models of the mode,
Faces which we meet everywhere

And necessary fools allowed.
Behold the dames who once were fine
With roses, caps and looks malign;
Some marriageable maids behold,
Blank, unapproachable and cold.
Lo, the ambassador who speaks
Economy political,
And with gray hair ambrosial
The old man who has had his freaks,
Renowned for his acumen, wit,
But now ridiculous a bit.

XXV

Behold Sabouroff, whom the age
For baseness of the spirit scorns,
Saint Priest, who every album's page
With blunted pencil-point adorns.
Another tribune of the ball
Hung like a print against the wall,
Pink as Palm Sunday cherubim,[84]

[84] On Palm Sunday the Russians carry branches, or used to do so. These branches

Motionless, mute, tight-laced and trim.
The traveller, bird of passage he,
Stiff, overstarched and insolent,
Awakens secret merriment
By his embarrassed dignity –
Mute glances interchanged aside
Meet punishment for him provide.

XXVI

But my Onéguine the whole eve
Within his mind Tattiana bore,
Not the young timid maid, believe,
Enamoured, simple-minded, poor,
But the indifferent princess,
Divinity without access
Of the imperial Neva's shore.
O Men, how very like ye are
To Eve the universal mother,
Possession hath no power to please,

---

were adorned with little painted pictures of cherubs with the ruddy complexions of tradition. Hence the comparison.

The serpent to unlawful trees
Aye bids ye in some way or other –
Unless forbidden fruit we eat,
Our paradise is no more sweet.

XXVII

Ah! how Tattiana was transformed,
How thoroughly her part she took!
How soon to habits she conformed
Which crushing dignity must brook!
Who would the maiden innocent
In the unmoved, magnificent
Autocrat of the drawing-room seek?
And he had made her heart beat quick!
'Twas he whom, amid nightly shades,
Whilst Morpheus his approach delays,
She mourned and to the moon would
  raise
The languid eye of love-sick maids,
Dreaming perchance in weal or woe
To end with him her path below.

XXVIII

To Love all ages lowly bend,
But the young unpolluted heart
His gusts should fertilize, amend,
As vernal storms the fields athwart.
Youth freshens beneath Passion's
  showers,
Develops and matures its powers,
And thus in season the rich field
Gay flowers and luscious fruit doth yield.
But at a later, sterile age,
The solstice of our earthly years,
Mournful Love's deadly trace appears
As storms which in chill autumn rage
And leave a marsh the fertile ground
And devastate the woods around.

XXIX

There was no doubt! Eugene, alas!
Tattiana loved as when a lad,
Both day and night he now must pass

In love-lorn meditation sad.
Careless of every social rule,
The crystals of her vestibule
He daily in his drives drew near
And like a shadow haunted her.
Enraptured was he if allowed
To swathe her shoulders in the furs,
If his hot hand encountered hers,
Or he dispersed the motley crowd
Of lackeys in her pathway grouped,
Or to pick up her kerchief stooped.

XXX

She seemed of him oblivious,
Despite the anguish of his breast,
Received him freely at her house,
At times three words to him addressed
In company, or simply bowed,
Or recognized not in the crowd.
No coquetry was there, I vouch –
Society endures not such!
Onéguine's cheek grew ashy pale,

Either she saw not or ignored;
Onéguine wasted; on my word,
Already he grew phthisical.
All to the doctors Eugene send,
And they the waters recommend.

XXXI

He went not – sooner was prepared
To write his forefathers to warn
Of his approach; but nothing cared
Tattiana – thus the sex is born. –
He obstinately will remain,
Still hopes, endeavours, though in vain.
Sickness more courage doth command
Than health, so with a trembling hand
A love epistle he doth scrawl.
Though correspondence as a rule
He used to hate – and was no fool –
Yet suffering emotional
Had rendered him an invalid;
But word for word his letter read.

Onéguine's Letter to Tattiana
All is foreseen. My secret drear
Will sound an insult in your ear.
What acrimonious scorn I trace
Depicted on your haughty face!
What do I ask? What cause assigned
That I to you reveal my mind?
To what malicious merriment,
It may be, I yield nutriment!

Meeting you in times past by chance,
Warmth I imagined in your glance,
But, knowing not the actual truth,
Restrained the impulses of youth;
Also my wretched liberty
I would not part with finally;
This separated us as well –
Lenski, unhappy victim, fell,
From everything the heart held dear
I then resolved my heart to tear;
Unknown to all, without a tie,
I thought – retirement, liberty,

Will happiness replace. My God!
How I have erred and felt the rod!

No, ever to behold your face,
To follow you in every place,
Your smiling lips, your beaming eyes,
To watch with lovers' ecstasies,
Long listen, comprehend the whole
Of your perfections in my soul,
Before you agonized to die –
This, this were true felicity!
But such is not for me. I brood
Daily of love in solitude.
My days of life approach their end,
Yet I in idleness expend
The remnant destiny concedes,
And thus each stubbornly proceeds.
I feel, allotted is my span;
But, that life longer may remain,
At morn I must assuredly
Know that thy face that day I see.

I tremble lest my humble prayer
You with stern countenance declare
The artifice of villany –
I hear your harsh, reproachful cry.
If ye but knew how dreadful 'tis
To bear love's parching agonies –
To burn, yet reason keep awake
The fever of the blood to slake –
A passionate desire to bend
And, sobbing at your feet, to blend
Entreaties, woes and prayers, confess
All that the heart would fain express –
Yet with a feigned frigidity
To arm the tongue and e'en the eye,
To be in conversation clear
And happy unto you appear.

So be it! But internal strife
I cannot longer wage concealed.
The die is cast! Thine is my life!
Into thy hands my fate I yield!

XXXII

No answer! He another sent.
Epistle second, note the third,
Remained unnoticed. Once he went
To an assembly – she appeared
Just as he entered. How severe!
She will not see, she will not hear.
Alas! she is as hard, behold,
And frosty as a Twelfth Night cold.
Oh, how her lips compressed restrain
The indignation of her heart!
A sidelong look doth Eugene dart:
Where, where, remorse, compassion,
  pain?
Where, where, the trace of tears?
  None, none!
Upon her brow sits wrath alone –

XXXIII

And it may be a secret dread
Lest the world or her lord divine

A certain little escapade
Well known unto Onéguine mine.
'Tis hopeless! Homeward doth he flee
Cursing his own stupidity,
And brooding o'er the ills he bore,
Society renounced once more.
Then in the silent cabinet
He in imagination saw
The time when Melancholy's claw
'Mid worldly pleasures chased him yet,
Caught him and by the collar took
And shut him in a lonely nook.

XXXIV

He read as vainly as before,
Perusing Gibbon and Rousseau,
Manzoni, Herder and Chamfort,[85]
Madame de Stael, Bichat, Tissot:

---

[85] Owing to the unstable nature of fame the names of some of the above literary worthies necessitate reference at this period in the nineteenth century.

He read the unbelieving Bayle,
Also the works of Fontenelle,
Some Russian authors he perused –
Nought in the universe refused:
Nor almanacs nor newspapers,
Which lessons unto us repeat,
Wherein I castigation get;
And where a madrigal occurs
Writ in my honour now and then –
E sempre bene, gentlemen!

[Johann Gottfried von Herder, b. 1744, d. 1803, a German philosopher, philanthropist and author, was the personal friend of Goethe and held the poet of court chaplain at Weimar. His chief work is entitled, "Ideas for a Philosophy of the History of Mankind," in 4 vols.

Sebastien Roch Nicholas Chamfort, b. 1741, d. 1794, was a French novelist and dramatist of the Revolution, who contrary to his real wishes became entangled in its meshes. He exercised a considerable influence over certain of its leaders, notably Mirabeau and Sieyès. He is said to have originated the title of the celebrated tract from the pen of the latter. "What is the Tiers Etat? Nothing. What ought it to be? Everything." He ultimately experienced the common destiny in those days, was thrown into prison and though shortly afterwards released, his incarceration had such an effect upon his mind that he committed suicide.

Marie Francois Xavier Bichat, b. 1771, d. 1802, a French anatomist and physiologist of eminence. His principal works are a "Traité des Membranes," "Anatomie générale appliquée à la Physiologie et à la Médecine," and "Recherches Physiologiques sur la Vie et la Mort." He died at an early age from constant exposure to noxious exhalations during his researches.

Pierre Francois Tissot, b. 1768, d. 1864, a French writer of the Revolution and Empire. In 1812 he was appointed by Napoleon editor of the **Gazette de France**. He wrote histories of the Revolution, of Napoleon and of France. He was likewise a poet and author of a work entitled "Les trois Irlandais Conjurés, ou l'ombre d'Emmet," and is believed to have edited Foy's "History of the Peninsular War."

The above catalogue by its heterogeneous composition gives a fair idea of the intellectual movement in Russia from the Empress Catherine the Second downwards. It is characterized by a feverish thirst for encyclopaedic knowledge without a corresponding power of assimilation.]

XXXV

But what results? His eyes peruse
But thoughts meander far away –
Ideas, desires and woes confuse
His intellect in close array.
His eyes, the printed lines betwixt,
On lines invisible are fixt;
'Twas these he read and these alone
His spirit was intent upon.
They were the wonderful traditions
Of kindly, dim antiquity,
Dreams with no continuity,

Prophecies, threats and apparitions,
The lively trash of stories long
Or letters of a maiden young.

XXXVI

And by degrees upon him grew
A lethargy of sense, a trance,
And soon imagination threw
Before him her wild game of chance.
And now upon the snow in thaw
A young man motionless he saw,
As one who bivouacs afield,
And heard a voice cry – **Why! He's killed!** –
And now he views forgotten foes,
Poltroons and men of slanderous tongue,
Bevies of treacherous maidens young;
Of thankless friends the circle rose,
A mansion – by the window, see!
She sits alone – 'tis ever **she!**

XXXVII

So frequently his mind would stray
He well-nigh lost the use of sense,
Almost became a poet say –
Oh! what had been his eminence!
Indeed, by force of magnetism
A Russian poem's mechanism
My scholar without aptitude
At this time almost understood.
How like a poet was my chum
When, sitting by his fire alone
Whilst cheerily the embers shone,
He "Benedetta" used to hum,
Or "Idol mio," and in the grate
Would lose his slippers or gazette.

XXXVIII

Time flies! a genial air abroad,
Winter resigned her empire white,
Onéguine ne'er as poet showed
Nor died nor lost his senses quite.
Spring cheered him up, and he resigned
His chambers close wherein confined

He marmot-like did hibernate,
His double sashes and his grate,
And sallied forth one brilliant morn –
Along the Neva's bank he sleighs,
On the blue blocks of ice the rays
Of the sun glisten; muddy, worn,
The snow upon the streets doth melt –
Whither along them doth he pelt?

XXXIX

Onéguine whither gallops? Ye
Have guessed already. Yes, quite so!
Unto his own Tattiana he,
Incorrigible rogue, doth go.
Her house he enters, ghastly white,
The vestibule finds empty quite –
He enters the saloon. 'Tis blank!
A door he opens. But why shrank
He back as from a sudden blow? –
Alone the princess sitteth there,
Pallid and with dishevelled hair,
Gazing upon a note below.

Her tears flow plentifully and
Her cheek reclines upon her hand.

XL

Oh! who her speechless agonies
Could not in that brief moment guess!
Who now could fail to recognize
Tattiana in the young princess!
Tortured by pangs of wild regret,
Eugene fell prostrate at her feet –
She starts, nor doth a word express,
But gazes on Onéguine's face
Without amaze or wrath displayed:
His sunken eye and aspect faint,
Imploring looks and mute complaint
She comprehends. The simple maid
By fond illusions once possest
Is once again made manifest.

XLI

His kneeling posture he retains –

Calmly her eyes encounter his –
Insensible her hand remains
Beneath his lips' devouring kiss.
What visions then her fancy thronged –
A breathless silence then, prolonged –
But finally she softly said:
"Enough, arise! for much we need
Without disguise ourselves explain.
Onéguine, hast forgotten yet
The hour when – Fate so willed – we met
In the lone garden and the lane?
How meekly then I heard you preach –
To-day it is my turn to teach.

XLII

"Onéguine, I was younger then,
And better, if I judge aright;
I loved you – what did I obtain?
Affection how did you requite?
But with austerity! – for you
No novelty – is it not true? –
Was the meek love a maiden feels.

But now – my very blood congeals,
Calling to mind your icy look
And sermon – but in that dread hour
I blame not your behaviour –
An honourable course ye took,
Displayed a noble rectitude –
My soul is filled with gratitude!

XLIII

“Then, in the country, is’t not true?
And far removed from rumour vain;
I did not please you. Why pursue
Me now, inflict upon me pain? –
Wherefore am I your quarry held? –
Is it that I am now compelled
To move in fashionable life,
That I am rich, a prince’s wife? –
Because my lord, in battles maimed,
Is petted by the Emperor? –
That my dishonour would ensure
A notoriety proclaimed,

And in society might shed
A bastard fame prohibited?

XLIV

"I weep. And if within your breast
My image hath not disappeared,
Know that your sarcasm ill-suppressed,
Your conversation cold and hard,
If the choice in my power were,
To lawless love I should prefer –
And to these letters and these tears.
For visions of my childish years
Then ye were barely generous,
Age immature averse to cheat –
But now – what brings you to my feet? –
How mean, how pusillanimous!
A prudent man like you and brave
To shallow sentiment a slave!

XLV

"Onéguine, all this sumptuousness,

The gilding of life's vanities,
In the world's vortex my success,
My splendid house and gaieties –
What are they? Gladly would I yield
This life in masquerade concealed,
This glitter, riot, emptiness,
For my wild garden and bookcase, –
Yes! for our unpretending home,
Onéguine – the beloved place
Where the first time I saw your face, –
Or for the solitary tomb
Wherein my poor old nurse doth lie
Beneath a cross and shrubbery.

XLVI

"'Twas possible then, happiness –
Nay, near – but destiny decreed –
My lot is fixed – with thoughtlessness
It may be that I did proceed –
With bitter tears my mother prayed,
And for Tattiana, mournful maid,
Indifferent was her future fate.

I married – now, I supplicate –
For ever your Tattiana leave.
Your heart possesses, I know well,
Honour and pride inflexible.
I love you – to what end deceive? –
But I am now another's bride –
For ever faithful will abide."

XLVII

She rose – departed. But Eugene
Stood as if struck by lightning fire.
What a storm of emotions keen
Raged round him and of balked desire!
And hark! the clank of spurs is heard
And Tania's husband soon appeared. –
But now our hero we must leave
Just at a moment which I grieve
Must be pronounced unfortunate –
For long – for ever. To be sure
Together we have wandered o'er
The world enough. Congratulate

Each other as the shore we climb!
Hurrah! it long ago was time!

XLVIII

Reader, whoever thou mayst be,
Foeman or friend, I do aspire
To part in amity with thee!
Adieu! whate'er thou didst desire
From careless stanzas such as these,
Of passion reminiscences,
Pictures of the amusing scene,
Repose from labour, satire keen,
Or faults of grammar on its page –
God grant that all who herein glance,
In serious mood or dalliance
Or in a squabble to engage,
May find a crumb to satisfy.
Now we must separate. Good-bye!

XLIX

And farewell thou, my gloomy friend,
Thou also, my ideal true,
And thou, persistent to the end,
My little book. With thee I knew
All that a poet could desire,
Oblivion of life's tempest dire,
Of friends the grateful intercourse –
Oh, many a year hath run its course
Since I beheld Eugene and young
Tattiana in a misty dream,
And my romance's open theme
Glittered in a perspective long,
And I discerned through Fancy's prism
Distinctly not its mechanism.

L

But ye to whom, when friendship heard,
The first-fruits of my tale I read,

As Saadi anciently averred – [86]
Some are afar and some are dead.
Without them Eugene is complete;
And thou, from whom Tattiana sweet;
Was drawn, ideal of my lay –
Ah! what hath fate not torn away!
Happy who quit life's banquet seat
Before the dregs they shall divine

---

[86] The celebrated Persian poet. Pushkin uses the passage referred to as an epigraph to the "Fountain of Baktchiserai." It runs thus: "Many, even as I, visited that fountain, but some of these are dead and some have journeyed afar." Saadi was born in 1189 at Shiraz and was a reputed descendant from Ali, Mahomet's son-in-law. In his youth he was a soldier, was taken prisoner by the Crusaders and forced to work in the ditches of Tripoli, whence he was ransomed by a merchant whose daughter he subsequently married. He did not commence writing till an advanced age. His principal work is the "Gulistan," or "Rose Garden," a work which has been translated into almost every European tongue.

Of the cup brimming o’er with wine –
Who the romance do not complete,
But who abandon it – as I
Have my Onéguine – suddenly.

END OF CANTO THE EIGHTH

www.ingramcontent.com/pod-product-compliance
Lightning Source LLC
Chambersburg PA
CBHW020915310726
48980CB00011B/890/J

* 9 7 8 1 8 3 4 1 2 2 6 1 8 *